Indian Philosophy: A Very Short Introduction

'an excellent short introduction which admirably fulfils its mission . . . This accessible volume is highly recommended for students of Indian thought and will also be very useful in courses on world philosophy.'

Damien Keown, University of London

'To present a clear introduction to Indian philosophy in 35,000 words is a challenging task, but few are better qualified to undertake it than Dr Hamilton. In this book she demonstrates not only her mastery of the field but also her gift for lucid and accurate exposition.'

Richard Gombrich, University of Oxford

Very Short Introductions available now:

ACCOUNTING Christopher Nobes
ADVERTISING Winston Fletcher
AFRICAN HISTORY John Parker and Richard Rathbone
AGNOSTICISM Robin Le Poidevin
ALEXANDER THE GREAT Hugh Bowden
AMERICAN HISTORY Paul S. Boyer
AMERICAN IMMIGRATION David A. Gerber
AMERICAN POLITICAL PARTIES AND ELECTIONS L. Sandy Maisel
AMERICAN POLITICS Richard M. Valelly
THE AMERICAN PRESIDENCY Charles O. Jones
ANAESTHESIA Aidan O'Donnell
ANARCHISM Colin Ward
ANCIENT EGYPT Ian Shaw
ANCIENT GREECE Paul Cartledge
THE ANCIENT NEAR EAST Amanda H. Podany
ANCIENT PHILOSOPHY Julia Annas
ANCIENT WARFARE Harry Sidebottom
ANGELS David Albert Jones
ANGLICANISM Mark Chapman
THE ANGLO-SAXON AGE John Blair
THE ANIMAL KINGDOM Peter Holland
ANIMAL RIGHTS David DeGrazia
THE ANTARCTIC Klaus Dodds
ANTISEMITISM Steven Beller
ANXIETY Daniel Freeman and Jason Freeman
THE APOCRYPHAL GOSPELS Paul Foster
ARCHAEOLOGY Paul Bahn
ARCHITECTURE Andrew Ballantyne
ARISTOCRACY William Doyle
ARISTOTLE Jonathan Barnes
ART HISTORY Dana Arnold
ART THEORY Cynthia Freeland
ASTROBIOLOGY David C. Catling
ATHEISM Julian Baggini
AUGUSTINE Henry Chadwick
AUSTRALIA Kenneth Morgan
AUTISM Uta Frith
THE AVANT GARDE David Cottington
THE AZTECS Davíd Carrasco
BACTERIA Sebastian G. B. Amyes
BARTHES Jonathan Culler
THE BEATS David Sterritt
BEAUTY Roger Scruton
BESTSELLERS John Sutherland
THE BIBLE John Riches
BIBLICAL ARCHAEOLOGY Eric H. Cline
BIOGRAPHY Hermione Lee
THE BLUES Elijah Wald
THE BOOK OF MORMON Terryl Givens
BORDERS Alexander C. Diener and Joshua Hagen
THE BRAIN Michael O'Shea
THE BRITISH CONSTITUTION Martin Loughlin
THE BRITISH EMPIRE Ashley Jackson
BRITISH POLITICS Anthony Wright
BUDDHA Michael Carrithers
BUDDHISM Damien Keown
BUDDHIST ETHICS Damien Keown
CANCER Nicholas James
CAPITALISM James Fulcher
CATHOLICISM Gerald O'Collins
CAUSATION Stephen Mumford and Rani Lill Anjum
THE CELL Terence Allen and Graham Cowling
THE CELTS Barry Cunliffe
CHAOS Leonard Smith
CHILDREN'S LITERATURE Kimberley Reynolds
CHINESE LITERATURE Sabina Knight
CHOICE THEORY Michael Allingham
CHRISTIAN ART Beth Williamson
CHRISTIAN ETHICS D. Stephen Long
CHRISTIANITY Linda Woodhead
CITIZENSHIP Richard Bellamy
CIVIL ENGINEERING David Muir Wood
CLASSICAL LITERATURE William Allan
CLASSICAL MYTHOLOGY Helen Morales
CLASSICS Mary Beard and John Henderson
CLAUSEWITZ Michael Howard
CLIMATE Mark Maslin
THE COLD WAR Robert McMahon
COLONIAL AMERICA Alan Taylor
COLONIAL LATIN AMERICAN LITERATURE Rolena Adorno
COMEDY Matthew Bevis
COMMUNISM Leslie Holmes
COMPLEXITY John H. Holland
THE COMPUTER Darrel Ince
THE CONQUISTADORS Matthew Restall and Felipe Fernández-Armesto
CONSCIENCE Paul Strohm
CONSCIOUSNESS Susan Blackmore
CONTEMPORARY ART Julian Stallabrass
CONTEMPORARY FICTION Robert Eaglestone
CONTINENTAL PHILOSOPHY Simon Critchley
CORAL REEFS Charles Sheppard
COSMOLOGY Peter Coles
CRITICAL THEORY Stephen Eric Bronner
THE CRUSADES Christopher Tyerman
CRYPTOGRAPHY Fred Piper and Sean Murphy
THE CULTURAL REVOLUTION Richard Curt Kraus
DADA AND SURREALISM David Hopkins
DARWIN Jonathan Howard
THE DEAD SEA SCROLLS Timothy Lim
DEMOCRACY Bernard Crick
DERRIDA Simon Glendinning
DESCARTES Tom Sorell
DESERTS Nick Middleton
DESIGN John Heskett
DEVELOPMENTAL BIOLOGY Lewis Wolpert
THE DEVIL Darren Oldridge
DIASPORA Kevin Kenny
DICTIONARIES Lynda Mugglestone
DINOSAURS David Norman
DIPLOMACY Joseph M. Siracusa
DOCUMENTARY FILM Patricia Aufderheide
DREAMING J. Allan Hobson
DRUGS Leslie Iversen
DRUIDS Barry Cunliffe
EARLY MUSIC Thomas Forrest Kelly
THE EARTH Martin Redfern
ECONOMICS Partha Dasgupta
EDUCATION Gary Thomas
EGYPTIAN MYTH Geraldine Pinch
EIGHTEENTH-CENTURY BRITAIN Paul Langford
THE ELEMENTS Philip Ball
EMOTION Dylan Evans
EMPIRE Stephen Howe
ENGELS Terrell Carver
ENGINEERING David Blockley
ENGLISH LITERATURE Jonathan Bate
ENVIRONMENTAL ECONOMICS Stephen Smith
EPIDEMIOLOGY Rodolfo Saracci
ETHICS Simon Blackburn

THE EUROPEAN UNION John Pinder and Simon Usherwood
EVOLUTION Brian and Deborah Charlesworth
EXISTENTIALISM Thomas Flynn
THE EYE Michael Land
FAMILY LAW Jonathan Herring
FASCISM Kevin Passmore
FASHION Rebecca Arnold
FEMINISM Margaret Walters
FILM Michael Wood
FILM MUSIC Kathryn Kalinak
THE FIRST WORLD WAR Michael Howard
FOLK MUSIC Mark Slobin
FOOD John Krebs
FORENSIC PSYCHOLOGY David Canter
FORENSIC SCIENCE Jim Fraser
FOSSILS Keith Thomson
FOUCAULT Gary Gutting
FRACTALS Kenneth Falconer
FREE SPEECH Nigel Warburton
FREE WILL Thomas Pink
FRENCH LITERATURE John D. Lyons
THE FRENCH REVOLUTION William Doyle
FREUD Anthony Storr
FUNDAMENTALISM Malise Ruthven
GALAXIES John Gribbin
GALILEO Stillman Drake
GAME THEORY Ken Binmore
GANDHI Bhikhu Parekh
GENIUS Andrew Robinson
GEOGRAPHY John Matthews and David Herbert
GEOPOLITICS Klaus Dodds
GERMAN LITERATURE Nicholas Boyle
GERMAN PHILOSOPHY Andrew Bowie
GLOBAL CATASTROPHES Bill McGuire
GLOBAL ECONOMIC HISTORY Robert C. Allen
GLOBAL WARMING Mark Maslin
GLOBALIZATION Manfred Steger
THE GOTHIC Nick Groom
GOVERNANCE Mark Bevir
THE GREAT DEPRESSION AND THE NEW DEAL Eric Rauchway
HABERMAS James Gordon Finlayson
HAPPINESS Daniel M. Haybron
HEGEL Peter Singer
HEIDEGGER Michael Inwood
HERODOTUS Jennifer T. Roberts
HIEROGLYPHS Penelope Wilson
HINDUISM Kim Knott
HISTORY John H. Arnold
THE HISTORY OF ASTRONOMY Michael Hoskin
THE HISTORY OF LIFE Michael Benton
THE HISTORY OF MATHEMATICS Jacqueline Stedall
THE HISTORY OF MEDICINE William Bynum
THE HISTORY OF TIME Leofranc Holford-Strevens
HIV/AIDS Alan Whiteside
HOBBES Richard Tuck
HORMONES Martin Luck
HUMAN EVOLUTION Bernard Wood
HUMAN RIGHTS Andrew Clapham
HUMANISM Stephen Law
HUME A. J. Ayer
HUMOUR Noël Carroll
THE ICE AGE Jamie Woodward
IDEOLOGY Michael Freeden
INDIAN PHILOSOPHY Sue Hamilton
INFORMATION Luciano Floridi
INNOVATION Mark Dodgson and David Gann
INTELLIGENCE Ian J. Deary
INTERNATIONAL MIGRATION Khalid Koser
INTERNATIONAL RELATIONS Paul Wilkinson
INTERNATIONAL SECURITY Christopher S. Browning
ISLAM Malise Ruthven
ISLAMIC HISTORY Adam Silverstein
ITALIAN LITERATURE Peter Hainsworth and David Robey
JESUS Richard Bauckham
JOURNALISM Ian Hargreaves
JUDAISM Norman Solomon
JUNG Anthony Stevens
KABBALAH Joseph Dan
KAFKA Ritchie Robertson
KANT Roger Scruton
KEYNES Robert Skidelsky
KIERKEGAARD Patrick Gardiner
THE KORAN Michael Cook
LANDSCAPE ARCHITECTURE Ian H. Thompson
LANDSCAPES AND GEOMORPHOLOGY Andrew Goudie and Heather Viles
LANGUAGES Stephen R. Anderson
LATE ANTIQUITY Gillian Clark
LAW Raymond Wacks
THE LAWS OF THERMODYNAMICS Peter Atkins
LEADERSHIP Keith Grint
LINCOLN Allen C. Guelzo
LINGUISTICS Peter Matthews
LITERARY THEORY Jonathan Culler
LOCKE John Dunn
LOGIC Graham Priest
MACHIAVELLI Quentin Skinner
MADNESS Andrew Scull
MAGIC Owen Davies
MAGNA CARTA Nicholas Vincent
MAGNETISM Stephen Blundell
MALTHUS Donald Winch
MANAGEMENT John Hendry
MAO Delia Davin
MARINE BIOLOGY Philip V. Mladenov
THE MARQUIS DE SADE John Phillips
MARTIN LUTHER Scott H. Hendrix
MARTYRDOM Jolyon Mitchell
MARX Peter Singer
MATHEMATICS Timothy Gowers
THE MEANING OF LIFE Terry Eagleton
MEDICAL ETHICS Tony Hope
MEDICAL LAW Charles Foster
MEDIEVAL BRITAIN John Gillingham and Ralph A. Griffiths
MEMORY Jonathan K. Foster
METAPHYSICS Stephen Mumford
MICHAEL FARADAY Frank A.J.L. James
MICROECONOMICS Avinash Dixit
MODERN ART David Cottington
MODERN CHINA Rana Mitter
MODERN FRANCE Vanessa R. Schwartz
MODERN IRELAND Senia Pašeta
MODERN JAPAN Christopher Goto-Jones
MODERN LATIN AMERICAN LITERATURE Roberto González Echevarría
MODERN WAR Richard English
MODERNISM Christopher Butler
MOLECULES Philip Ball
THE MONGOLS Morris Rossabi
MORMONISM Richard Lyman Bushman
MUHAMMAD Jonathan A.C. Brown

MULTICULTURALISM Ali Rattansi
MUSIC Nicholas Cook
MYTH Robert A. Segal
THE NAPOLEONIC WARS Mike Rapport
NATIONALISM Steven Grosby
NELSON MANDELA Elleke Boehmer
NEOLIBERALISM Manfred Steger and Ravi Roy
NETWORKS Guido Caldarelli and Michele Catanzaro
THE NEW TESTAMENT Luke Timothy Johnson
THE NEW TESTAMENT AS LITERATURE Kyle Keefer
NEWTON Robert Iliffe
NIETZSCHE Michael Tanner
NINETEENTH-CENTURY BRITAIN Christopher Harvie and H. C. G. Matthew
THE NORMAN CONQUEST George Garnett
NORTH AMERICAN INDIANS Theda Perdue and Michael D. Green
NORTHERN IRELAND Marc Mulholland
NOTHING Frank Close
NUCLEAR POWER Maxwell Irvine
NUCLEAR WEAPONS Joseph M. Siracusa
NUMBERS Peter M. Higgins
NUTRITION David A. Bender
OBJECTIVITY Stephen Gaukroger
THE OLD TESTAMENT Michael D. Coogan
THE ORCHESTRA D. Kern Holoman
ORGANIZATIONS Mary Jo Hatch
PAGANISM Owen Davies
THE PALESTINIAN-ISRAELI CONFLICT Martin Bunton
PARTICLE PHYSICS Frank Close
PAUL E. P. Sanders
PENTECOSTALISM William K. Kay
THE PERIODIC TABLE Eric R. Scerri
PHILOSOPHY Edward Craig
PHILOSOPHY OF LAW Raymond Wacks
PHILOSOPHY OF SCIENCE Samir Okasha
PHOTOGRAPHY Steve Edwards
PLAGUE Paul Slack
PLANETS David A. Rothery
PLANTS Timothy Walker
PLATO Julia Annas
POLITICAL PHILOSOPHY David Miller
POLITICS Kenneth Minogue
POSTCOLONIALISM Robert Young
POSTMODERNISM Christopher Butler
POSTSTRUCTURALISM Catherine Belsey
PREHISTORY Chris Gosden
PRESOCRATIC PHILOSOPHY Catherine Osborne
PRIVACY Raymond Wacks
PROBABILITY John Haigh
PROGRESSIVISM Walter Nugent
PROTESTANTISM Mark A. Noll
PSYCHIATRY Tom Burns
PSYCHOLOGY Gillian Butler and Freda McManus
PURITANISM Francis J. Bremer
THE QUAKERS Pink Dandelion
QUANTUM THEORY John Polkinghorne
RACISM Ali Rattansi
RADIOACTIVITY Claudio Tuniz
RASTAFARI Ennis B. Edmonds
THE REAGAN REVOLUTION Gil Troy
REALITY Jan Westerhoff
THE REFORMATION Peter Marshall
RELATIVITY Russell Stannard
RELIGION IN AMERICA Timothy Beal
THE RENAISSANCE Jerry Brotton
RENAISSANCE ART Geraldine A. Johnson
REVOLUTIONS Jack A. Goldstone
RHETORIC Richard Toye
RISK Baruch Fischhoff and John Kadvany
RIVERS Nick Middleton
ROBOTICS Alan Winfield
ROMAN BRITAIN Peter Salway
THE ROMAN EMPIRE Christopher Kelly
THE ROMAN REPUBLIC David M. Gwynn
ROMANTICISM Michael Ferber
ROUSSEAU Robert Wokler
RUSSELL A. C. Grayling
RUSSIAN HISTORY Geoffrey Hosking
RUSSIAN LITERATURE Catriona Kelly
THE RUSSIAN REVOLUTION S. A. Smith
SCHIZOPHRENIA Chris Frith and Eve Johnstone
SCHOPENHAUER Christopher Janaway
SCIENCE AND RELIGION Thomas Dixon
SCIENCE FICTION David Seed
THE SCIENTIFIC REVOLUTION Lawrence M. Principe
SCOTLAND Rab Houston
SEXUALITY Véronique Mottier
SHAKESPEARE Germaine Greer
SIKHISM Eleanor Nesbitt
THE SILK ROAD James A. Millward
SLEEP Steven W. Lockley and Russell G. Foster
SOCIAL AND CULTURAL ANTHROPOLOGY John Monaghan and Peter Just
SOCIALISM Michael Newman
SOCIOLINGUISTICS John Edwards
SOCIOLOGY Steve Bruce
SOCRATES C. C. W. Taylor
THE SOVIET UNION Stephen Lovell
THE SPANISH CIVIL WAR Helen Graham
SPANISH LITERATURE Jo Labanyi
SPINOZA Roger Scruton
SPIRITUALITY Philip Sheldrake
STARS Andrew King
STATISTICS David J. Hand
STEM CELLS Jonathan Slack
STUART BRITAIN John Morrill
SUPERCONDUCTIVITY Stephen Blundell
SYMMETRY Ian Stewart
TEETH Peter S. Ungar
TERRORISM Charles Townshend
THEOLOGY David F. Ford
THOMAS AQUINAS Fergus Kerr
THOUGHT Tim Bayne
TIBETAN BUDDHISM Matthew T. Kapstein
TOCQUEVILLE Harvey C. Mansfield
TRAGEDY Adrian Poole
THE TROJAN WAR Eric H. Cline
TRUST Katherine Hawley
THE TUDORS John Guy
TWENTIETH-CENTURY BRITAIN Kenneth O. Morgan
THE UNITED NATIONS Jussi M. Hanhimäki
THE U.S. CONGRESS Donald A. Ritchie
THE U.S. SUPREME COURT Linda Greenhouse
UTOPIANISM Lyman Tower Sargent
THE VIKINGS Julian Richards
VIRUSES Dorothy H. Crawford
WITCHCRAFT Malcolm Gaskill
WITTGENSTEIN A. C. Grayling
WORK Stephen Fineman
WORLD MUSIC Philip Bohlman
THE WORLD TRADE ORGANIZATION Amrita Narlikar
WRITING AND SCRIPT Andrew Robinson

Sue Hamilton

INDIAN PHILOSOPHY

A Very Short Introduction

OXFORD
UNIVERSITY PRESS

OXFORD
UNIVERSITY PRESS

Great Clarendon Street, Oxford OX2 6DP

Oxford University Press is a department of the University of Oxford.
It furthers the University's objective of excellence in research, scholarship,
and education by publishing worldwide in

Oxford New York

Auckland Bangkok Buenos Aires Cape Town Chennai
Dar es Salaam Delhi Hong Kong Istanbul Karachi Kolkata
Kuala Lumpur Madrid Melbourne Mexico City Mumbai Nairobi
São Paulo Shanghai Taipei Tokyo Toronto

Published in the United States
by Oxford University Press Inc., New York

First published as an Oxford University Press paperback 2000
First published as a Very Short Introduction 2001

British Library Cataloging in Publication Data
Data available

Library of Congress Cataloguing in Publication Data
Data available

ISBN 978-0-19-285374-5

20

Typeset by RefineCatch Ltd, Bungay, Suffolk
Printed in Great Britain by
Ashford Colour Press Ltd, Gosport, Hants.

Contents

List of illustrations

List of maps

Preface

Indian philosophy in 35,000 words? Many would consider it impossible! And it is certain that of those who might be persuaded to attempt it, no two would handle it in the same way. My own approach to the diversity of the material for the purposes of this book is explained in Chapter 1. In any case, the primary aims of a very short introduction are to give a flavour, to lead the interested reader into a larger and more complex topic than the book can cover comprehensively, to make such a topic accessible to the beginner. These have been my guidelines. I hope that this book is also thought-provoking, both in introducing very different ways of thinking about the world we experience, and in the sense of nudging those who are interested towards further investigation of the subject. To this end, a list of recommended further reading is included at the end of the book.

When discussing philosophical thought in an introductory way, and working from non-English texts, one has to deal with two practical problems: the need to use technical terms associated with philosophical issues, and how best to translate key words and textual extracts. Technical terms I have tried to keep to an absolute minimum, but explanatory text boxes have been given where their usage is important enough to require the beginner to acquire familiarity with them. It should in any case be remembered that the terms themselves are less important than gaining an understanding of what they are referring to.

When it comes to translating, sometimes a key word is not translatable into meaningful English, and in such cases I have left it in its original Sanskrit or Pāli. I would ask the reader not to be put off by the unfamiliarity of these words. Most disciplines and subject areas – such as Latin, Greek, and works on other major linguistic or cultural traditions, mathematics and physics, and nowadays technology and computing – require the accepting and learning of a few key terms that initially might seem alien. In this book, the number of untranslated words is small, and in each case I think the clear context in which they are used will help the reader understand them.

When it comes to quoting longer extracts from primary texts, a greater problem is how literally one translates them. Not only does faithfulness to the grammar and syntax of the original frequently result in awkward and stilted English, and not only do many component words simply not have a meaningful English equivalent: it is also the case that literalness often fails to convey the point of what was being said. On balance, I think it is preferable to attempt to transpose original passages into meaningful English wherever possible. I have therefore tried to use ordinary English in contemporary style, and in the interests of clarity have not refrained in some cases from paraphrasing rather than more formally translating. My purpose overall has been to convey the conceptual point(s) of the extract as clearly as possible. If they wish to, readers may consult other published translations of the texts either for comparison or for alternative treatments of the material. In this book all translations or paraphrases are my own unless otherwise stated.

I would like to thank George Miller of Oxford University Press for inviting me to write this book, and for his gentle guidance and suggestions. Thanks also to Tracy Miller for invaluable advice during the editing process. And I am particularly grateful to King's College, London for allowing me to take sabbatical leave to write this book at a time when all academics are under enormous pressure to publish quantities of 'primary research'.

Very many thanks, too, to Muriel Anderson, Cecilia Storr, and Gay Watson for generously giving their time to read and comment on the draft manuscript. I accept full responsibility for the final version. To Richard Gombrich, colleague and friend, thank you for untold advice, criticism and support, not just in respect of this one project. And to Clare Palmer, for so long a wonderful sounding board and exchanger of ideas and thoughts, page 107 is especially for you.

A Note on Languages and Pronunciation

Two languages used by the Indian tradition are referred to in this book, Sanskrit and Pāli. As is explained in early chapters, the tradition began when people who called themselves Aryans migrated from central Eurasia into the north of India, by way of what is now Pakistan, many hundreds of years BCE. The language in which they preserved their ritual practices was Sanskrit, which at a later date was codified into its 'classical' form by a grammarian called Pāṇini (see Chapter 4). In the history of languages, Sanskrit is known as 'old Indo-Aryan', and it is the language in which most Indian philosophical material was written. Over time, alongside classical Sanskrit, variant and more vernacular forms of the language emerged, now collectively known as 'middle Indo-Aryan' languages. One of these is Pāli, the language in which many of the earliest Buddhist texts are preserved. The close link between the languages is illustrated in the Sanskrit word *dharma*, which is *dhamma* in Pāli; *nirvāṇa* becomes *nibbāna* (or 'nirvana' in its Anglicized form).

Both Sanskrit and Pāli are phonetic languages based on the same alphabet. This is somewhat longer than the Roman alphabet with which we are familiar, and many of the extra letters are represented with what are called 'diacritic marks': for example ā as well as a; ñ, ṇ, and ṅ as well as n; ś and ṣ as well as s. Sometimes one finds English works transposing, say, ś into sh, because this is how ś sounds. Pronunciation is more accurate, however, if the diacritic marks are retained, so I have chosen to use the full Sanskrit and Pāli alphabet in this book.

Familiarizing oneself with the pronunciation can help in overcoming any initial feeling of strangeness, so here are some pronunciation guidelines.

a	short, as in h*u*t
ā	long, as in nirv*a*na
i	short, as in h*i*t
ī	long, as in f*ee*t
u	short, as in p*u*t
ū	long, as in b*oo*t
e	sounds like m*ay*
o	sounds like rope
ṛ	as in p*r*etty
s	as in *s*it
ś, ṣ	variations on *sh*
ñ	as in ca*ny*on
ṅ, ṇ	as in *n*ot, with n sounded with the tongue at the back of the palate
t	as in *t*ea
ṭ	as in *t*ea, but with t sounded with the tongue at the back of the palate
ṃ	as in ha*ng*
k, g	always hard – as in *k*ill, *g*ull
c, j	always soft – as in *ch*ill, *j*ug
h	is always sounded – as in up*h*ill (so Budd*h*a)
r	is always sounded, as in Irish or American English (so ka*r*ma; *kāma* means 'desire' – as in Kāma Sūtra)

Practising on a few examples can help in the familiarization process, so try the following:

> ṛṣi, Himālaya, dhamma, saṃsāra, Nāgārjuna, Bhartṛhari, ānvīkṣikī, ātman, Mīmāṃsā, *darśana*, *mokṣa*, Vaiśeṣika, Śaṅkara, Sāṃkhya, Viśiṣṭa-ādvaita-vedānta

Chapter 1
Reason and Belief
Richness and diversity in Indian thought

India has a long, rich, and diverse tradition of philosophical thought, spanning some two and a half millennia and encompassing several major religious traditions. Religion in the context of philosophy is particularly significant because traditionally in India it is believed that the role of philosophizing, in the sense of attempting to understand the nature of whatever it is one is focusing on, is directly associated with one's personal destiny. So philosophy is seen not in terms of a professional intellectual pursuit that can be set aside at the end of the working day, but as an attempt to understand the true nature of reality in terms of an inner or spiritual quest. One might say that what Westerners call religion and philosophy are combined in India in people's attempts to understand the meaning and structure of life – in the broadest sense. This is comparable more with the approach of Socrates than with religion as faith in revelation and philosophy as an academic discipline.

Thinking and Believing

This point about the nature of Indian philosophy is an important one to grasp at the outset, so it is worth exploring it further. In the West, certainly since the great German philosopher Immanuel Kant separated God from what he thought could be learned about the nature of things by means of reasoning, there has been a clear divide between philosophy and religion. Religion has been seen as a field in which 'leaps of faith' are not just permitted but sometimes *required*; primacy may be given to what certain people state to be the case simply because of who they are (that is to say, what they say is taken as true regardless of whether or not it is demonstrably, or even arguably, true); and varying degrees of 'otherness' are found, such as a transcendent God, beings whose status and/or knowledge is in some sense superhuman or supernatural, and/or various kinds of superhuman or supernatural power source(s). All or any of such factors are 'believed' by adherents of the different religious traditions, either unquestioningly or within a questioning framework, and as such these people are known as 'believers'.

A key point for believers is that they also believe that practising their religion is directly linked with their destiny. The details of this relationship vary. Some think their lives here and now are affected by their religious beliefs and practices. Others think the effects are experienced only after death. Some believe that what happens to them now and/or after death is brought about directly by their own beliefs and practices, some that their destiny is entirely in the hands of whatever transcendent, superhumanly powerful 'other' they believe in, and some that it is a combination of these two. However the details are understood, the existence of this relationship between religious beliefs and practices and the individual's destiny – particularly after death – is why religions are referred to as soteriologies, or 'systems of salvation'.

Religion as soteriology: from the Greek word *soter* meaning 'saviour'. In common usage, it is not necessary for a system to hold that there is an actual saviour figure for the system itself to be termed a soteriology. The key point is that the destiny of the believers in question is thought to be directly connected with their beliefs and practices.

In contrast to this, since Kant the discipline of philosophy has been primarily concerned with the investigation of what can be known of the nature and structure of reality by means of rational argument alone. That is to say, whatever specific topics philosophers concern themselves with, the way they do it must be logically watertight: no leaps of faith are permitted, no one's word is privileged over rationality, and no part of the exercise is anything other than a human intellectual endeavour. Furthermore, philosophizing, whatever it is about, is considered purely as an intellectual end in itself, and may have no effect on one whatsoever. Philosophy is simply not soteriological – indeed, that is an important aspect of what distinguishes it from religion.

Two things are notable about this divide between religion and philosophy. The first is that, in spite of their differences, the two fields share a number of common interests. The second is that even in the West the distinction between the two was not always so clear cut. The commonality lies in the fact that both religion and philosophy are fundamentally concerned with the nature of reality. As an example, let us consider a religion with the following teachings: there is a being that it calls God, that is wholly transcendent of the cosmos as we know it; God is the creator of all things; the created realm includes human beings with eternal souls; one's behaviour has an effect on one's afterlife. Even from this minimal amount of information we know that according to this religion, reality is comprised of two absolutely distinct kinds of being (in this case, God, and not-God), and that there cannot be anything else, because God is the creator of all things. We also know that at least part of what is not-God is both plural (all the individual souls) and everlasting. Less abstractly, this last point tells us something important about the nature of human beings, in themselves a part of reality that might be comprised in any of a number of ways. And in addition to this, we know that some kind of system of causation links present behaviour to an unknown future mode of existence.

Even though there are many other aspects of the nature of reality one might be interested in knowing, and about which the religion might also have something to say, and despite the generality of this example, what we have here deals with two of the key issues with which philosophy is also concerned: how reality is fundamentally constituted, and the nature of the human being.

Another issue of common concern to religion and philosophy is how one arrives at knowing the answers to such key questions. If, in the case of our hypothetical religion, the teaching is given by a superhuman being whose word is accepted as true by believers, then one's knowledge is acquired through 'revelation', or what might be called 'verbal testimony'. In fact, we all rely on verbal testimony a great deal in our everyday lives. Those of us who have never travelled to Antarctica, for example, accept as true the account of those who have seen it that it is where the maps locate it. That childbirth is painful is accepted by those who have not experienced it on the word of those who have. And all of us regularly learn of all kinds of things on the basis of the testimony of news reporters, teachers, writers, scientists, expert researchers, and so on. In everyday situations, the information acquired in such a way can, at least in principle, be checked. What makes the religious situation different is not the means of knowing, but that the topics are not open to being checked. So the information given by the religious teacher can only be accepted on trust, or 'believed'. A philosopher would consider this uncheckability unacceptable and would not regard such information about the nature of reality as valid. Working on the same topics, a philosopher would rely only on processes of knowing that are rational or logical. The discipline of philosophy thus specifically concerns itself with what are known as the 'limits of knowledge'. That is to say, it seeks to establish the criteria according to which data can and cannot legitimately be understood to be valid knowledge. Theories of knowledge (how we know) are referred to as epistemology.

With regard to the second point mentioned above, that there was not always such a clear-cut separation of what is religious and what is

Of interest to both religion and philosophy

Metaphysics concerns the nature of reality as a whole. It questions how reality is fundamentally constituted, and the types and natures of, and relationship between, any constituents there may be. The world/universe/cosmos, human beings, other beings, and causation are all important areas of interest.

Epistemology (from the Greek *episteme*, meaning 'knowledge') is about means of knowing. Common means of knowing include logical argument or reasoning, inference, testimony, perception.

philosophical, the Western philosophical tradition began in pre-Christian Greece, in a milieu and at a time when many were seeking to know more about the nature of reality. The aim and purpose then was to achieve wisdom in this respect, and any relevant insight was conceived of in terms of becoming wise: hence philosophy – 'love of wisdom'. Philosophizing incorporated no concept of soteriology as we understand it. But the various hypotheses about the nature of reality put forward by the great Greek philosophers nevertheless covered issues that might also be found as part of religious teachings. They concerned themselves with the nature of the world and the human being, and of the importance for the human being of seeking to become wise. This was seen as the highest possible activity for a human being, which should be aspired to if at all possible. Suggestions were also made, notably by Socrates, as to how one might combine the quest for wisdom with living an optimally good life.

After the Greeks, Western philosophy in the Christian era was for many centuries dominated by people who were also profoundly religious, and who were seeking to understand more about 'God's world'. Philosophers of great original insight and influence such as Augustine, Anselm, Aquinas, Descartes, and Hegel were all practising Christians, and sought to resolve rather than separate religious and philosophical issues. While the interests of these great thinkers were extremely wide-ranging, one issue that was of particular concern was how God fitted into the structure of reality. The existence of God as understood by the Christian tradition was taken as axiomatically true as an article of faith, but attempts were also made to establish his existence by means of rational argument. In this way, faith would be in harmony, rather than at odds, with reason. It was also argued, notably by Descartes, that the nature of God was such that one might safely rely on his assistance in overcoming the limitations of reasoning alone. Faith thus combined with reason in the quest for understanding, and indeed extended the possibilities of understanding. Such philosophers were well aware of what they were doing, but believed their approach a wholly legitimate one. The first philosopher in the Christian West seriously to question the legitimacy of mixing faith and reason in the quest for knowledge was Kant. Kant insisted that what one could know for certain was strictly limited to what could be ascertained by means of reasoning, and this did not include anything to do with God. As a devout Christian, Kant believed God existed. But he separated that belief from philosophical logic, and stated that one could never have certain knowledge about issues of faith; these were and would always remain beliefs, and certain knowledge was the province of philosophy.

Thus the Western philosophical tradition nowadays purports to concern itself only with certain knowledge and investigates only those issues that can be considered by means of logical argument. So rigidly has this methodological criterion come to be imposed that since the early 20th century the majority of philosophers have not concerned themselves with big metaphysical questions such as What is there? What exists? What is the absolute truth about the nature of reality? Some would say that addressing such questions involves deductions too speculative to be safely within the bounds of possible intelligibility and so the issues are best left alone. Others maintain that questions relating to anything that might extend beyond empirical human experience are intrinsically nonsensical. Modern philosophy thus tends to be concerned with detailed and technical questions about kinds of logic and linguistic analysis. Topics such as ethics and goodness, that earlier philosophers had discussed in the context of how they should live their own lives as they sought wisdom or understanding, tend to be considered and argued for as intellectual abstractions. Professional philosophy has become separated from the personal quest, and for many philosophy per se is understood only in this modern sense.

In approaching the origins and development of the Indian philosophical tradition, one needs to understand the role of philosophizing more in its traditional or original sense, as described above, rather than as it has come to be understood in the modern period. Philosophy in India is about seeking to understand the nature of reality. Furthermore, the point of doing this is that it is believed that understanding reality has a profound effect on one's destiny. For some the goal is straightforwardly soteriological, for others less so; but for all it is what we would call a spiritual undertaking, an activity associated with a religious tradition. Indeed, the distinction we make between religion and philosophy would simply not have been understood in India until very recent times, when Western missionaries and academics began forcing apart the various features of the Indian traditions in order that they might more readily be accommodated within their own Western conceptual framework.

Before elaborating some of the features of the Indian context, a word of caution: perhaps because of the overlap between philosophy and religion in India, there is a tendency in the West to regard its thinking as 'mystical', even 'magical', in contrast to the 'rationality' of the West. This is a mistake. Such a view derives from romanticizing thought-systems that originate elsewhere and present themselves differently, and attributing various 'exotic' connotations to what is merely unfamiliar. There is in fact a strong tradition of rational argument in India, and this has been as important to the proponents of the various systems of thought there as it has been to the great philosophers of the West.

Westerners approaching the Indian tradition for the first time, whether their interest be primarily in religion or in philosophy, are faced with two equal and opposite problems. One is to find something graspable amid the apparently bewildering multiplicity; the other is not enforcing such a straitjacket onto the material as to overlook significant aspects of the diversity. The classic example of the latter is 'Hinduism': because of the existence of the name Hinduism, Westerners expect to find a monolithic tradition comparable to other 'isms'. They remain baffled by what they find until they discover that Hinduism is a label that was attached in the 19th century to a highly complex and multiple collection of systems of thought by other Westerners who did not appreciate that complexity. Imagine the area covered by Europe and the Middle East at the time of the beginning of the Common Era – and suppose that outsiders had attached a single label to 'the religion' of that time and area. This will give an idea of what happened when 'the religion' of India was labelled Hinduism, and the extent of what needs to be unpacked to understand the tradition in its own terms.

But just as the many different aspects of European and Middle Eastern religion and thought have certain common origins, themes, and structures, and just as they to a great extent share a worldview and conceptual framework, so this is the case in India. What one has to do in order to unravel the complexity and make it graspable, then, is to find those common origins, themes, and structures, and to familiarize oneself with the worldview and conceptual framework within which Indian thought operates. Fortunately for such an enterprise, India has its own equivalent of an ancient Greek period, when its philosophical tradition began. Though these early Indian thinkers were drawing on and developing even earlier ideas and material, some of which we know about, it was during the 5th century BCE that clearly identifiable schools of thought began to acknowledge each other, interacting, debating, seeking to refute, and sometimes merging. It was from this period that different approaches coexisted, some remaining within the tradition that some two millennia later was retrospectively labelled 'Hinduism', and some establishing other traditions, such as Buddhism and Jainism. This early period will be the subject of Chapters 2 and 3.

Insight of the Truth

Traditionally, an Indian philosophy is referred to as a *darśana*, and this term itself gives us some indication of an underlying aspect of the worldview and conceptual framework within which Indian philosophical thought operates. Darśana literally means 'view', in the sense of having a cognitive 'sight' of something. What is implicit in this is that what is 'viewed' or 'sighted' is the truth about the nature of reality, and this reflects the fact that understanding the nature of reality is the aim of philosophizing in India. The original teachers associated with specific darśanas were referred to as *ṛṣis* (rishis), which means 'seers'.

Leading on from this, the term darśana also indicates that it is widely accepted that human beings are able to gain an actual sighting, in the sense of experiential knowledge, of metaphysical truth. Insight, or wisdom as it is sometimes called in English, in Indian thought is not restricted to intellectual knowledge. While rational argument and intellectual debate play an extremely important part in the philosophies of India – in some, almost to the exclusion of other factors – it is also accepted that, by means of mental disciplinary exercises of various kinds, one's cognitive perception can be developed and changed so that one can see in ways that transcend what one is 'normally' capable of. We shall see that some specific darśanas base their teachings and arguments on what ancient seers have stated to be the case from their own metaphysical insights, and the testimony of those seers is taken as having absolute validity – as valid as if one had seen it for oneself, or as if the point had been arrived at by means of logical argument alone. For others, the point is that the teaching of the darśana is such that anyone following it should themselves be able to 'see' the truth it teaches. In principle, the ability to gain metaphysical insight is thought to be a universal human characteristic; it is not that those who claim to do so are regarded as in some sense superhuman. Reorienting one's cognitive faculties so that such insight is possible is the rationale underlying the practice of yoga, and the resulting insight is called yogic perception.

This is one of the most profound differences between the worldview in which Indian thought operates and the worldview of the West, and perhaps the one that Westerners find most difficult to empathize with. It is perhaps because of this that Western philosophers tend to focus only on those aspects of Indian philosophy concerned with issues of logical argument, and it may also have contributed to why others attribute magical or mystical qualities to Indian thought. From the perspective of the Indian worldview, though, the possibility of changing one's cognitive perception is something to be regarded as systematically possible by means of regular disciplinary exercises in a manner not all that different from systematically acquiring the ability to play a musical instrument. Both require long-term perseverance and practice and involve the fine-tuning of various aspects of bodily and mental coordination. There is nothing magical about either – both are regarded as skills.

Karma and Rebirth

Karma and rebirth are other characteristic aspects of the Indian worldview. Karma is the Anglicized form of the Sanskrit word *karman*, which literally means 'action'. Implicit in the way the term is used is that actions have consequences, and karma refers to this action–consequence mechanics, operating as a natural law. The term itself is entirely neutral and different traditions append values to it in different ways. Similarly, the locus of the action–consequence mechanism varies in different traditions. The rationale of karma as actions having consequences originated in the actions associated with sacrificial rituals, the performance of which was believed to bring about certain specific consequences that contributed to the optimum functioning of the cosmos. The ritual actions to which consequences were linked were either physical or verbal (making a sound was an 'act'), and accuracy was essential if the mechanics were to be efficacious. Thus what made an action right or good was its correctness, and the values associated with such an understanding of karma were not moral ones.

By the 5th century BCE, alongside this earliest understanding of karma, it was also being taught that living one's life according to duties prescribed by religious teachers – the 'acting out' of duties: including, but not limited to, the performing of sacrificial rituals – would have beneficial consequences for individuals themselves. At this stage, karma came to be associated with the idea of rebirth, as it was believed that the consequences, positive or negative, of how one had performed one's duties, might be experienced in any one of many future lives, the conditions of each of which would be determined in this way. As with karma as ritual action, the linking of consequences to the performing of prescribed duties also carried a value criterion of correctness and not morality. At a later stage in the development of this branch of the Indian religious tradition, this point was emphasized when important teachers reiterated that it was better to do one's own duty badly than another's duty well; and better unquestioningly to do one's duty, however seemingly amoral it might be, than to neglect it on the basis of moral principle.

Other interpretations of the mechanics of karma that were taught during the 5th century BCE included those of the Jains and the Buddhists. The Jains stated that all actions – which they classified as verbal, physical, and mental – caused particles of matter to stick to one's soul, and it was this that weighed it down and kept it being reborn in the cycle of rebirth. Because Jains also believed that one should strive to free one's soul from this predicament, their teaching implied that all karma is bad karma: there can be no 'good' consequence of an action. In contrast, according to the Buddha the operating of karma is radically moral, in that what brings about a consequence is one's intention. As far as the law of karma is concerned, one's intentions, the Buddha stated, *are* one's actions: it is not what one does outwardly and visibly that counts but the state of one's mind. So here the karmic mechanism is not located in what is normally meant by 'actions'.

Karma, then, is the operation of an action-has-consequence mechanics. While it is differently interpreted by different schools of thought, it is nevertheless a fundamental part of the Indian worldview as a whole, accepted by all but a relatively small school of radical materialists. And since the 5th century BCE the notion of karma has generally been associated with the belief that individuals experience successive rebirths. The action–consequence mechanism acts as the fuel of the continuity of rebirth, and the specific conditions of each rebirth are linked to the specifics of earlier actions.

This aspect of the Indian worldview is important for us to grasp mainly because of the way in which it is associated with insight into the true nature of reality. Most Indian systems of thought teach that gaining such insight brings about the liberation of the individual from karmic continuity. This is the main aim and purpose of the philosophizing imperative and why 'philosophy' is associated with 'religion'. In presenting its 'view' of the truth, each darśana is as it were describing what it is that its practitioners will 'see'. And the importance of the goal – what Westerners would call 'salvation' – explains why each school of thought considered it so important to establish the coherence, validity, and efficacy of its teachings.

Complexity and Variety: Choosing the Content

The polemical environment that evolved over time, in which competing worldviews were debated, was highly complex and original, multi-stranded, and varied. This means that in a very short introduction difficult choices have to be made as to what is included and what omitted. Notable omissions in this book include Jainism, mentioned above. Mahāvīra, the founder of Jainism, was a contemporary of the Buddha. His teachings were original and interesting, and the tradition has not been without influence in the Indian religio-philosophical tradition, but the omission can nevertheless be made without doing violence to the broader tradition as a whole. The Cārvāka tradition, which systematized a materialistic school of thought, is also omitted, except in passing. Its importance lay in its formulation of challenges to opposing schools of thought, and it made interesting contributions to the milieu of philosophical debate. As with Jainism, however, omitting extensive discussion of it does not raise problems in understanding the broader picture. Another major omission is Śaivism. Śaivism represents an important, sophisticated, and highly influential strand of Indian thought, but it embraces so extensive and internally various a field that a very brief treatment of it would serve only to distort it.

As well as omitting these important traditions, a book of this nature does not allow for any detailed account of the way each of the various philosophical schools of thought developed and branched internally over time, usually as a result of different interpretations of their own seminal ideas and key texts. This was extremely common in the polemical climate in which the traditions flourished, as adherents of each school sought new ways of rejecting the claims of others without diverging from their own primary sources. The nature of these sources also meant that different interpretations of them were in any case likely. Often this was because they were recorded in very brief and/or cryptic style, requiring an expert or teacher to pass on to a student their full meaning. Sometimes, for example in the case of schools of thought based on exegesis of texts called the Upaniṣads, it was because the textual material was so extensive that different approaches and differences of emphasis produced quite different overall interpretations. Where the key features of major branches of a tradition can be clearly and concisely presented, these are included. But for an account of the vast majority of detailed developments the reader is advised to consult a more comprehensive work.

> *Exegesis* is the interpretation of textual material. Different exegetes might interpret the same material differently. That is, they might each claim a different meaning from the same text or passage. This allows for the subsequent drawing out of sometimes very different implications from the same core source.

What this book focuses on is, first, an account of the period during which the Indian religio-philosophical tradition identifiably began, the 5th century BCE, and the key features of the dominant ideas and practices of the time. Why certain issues emerged as being of crucial importance to particular schools of thought is discussed, helping to contextualize the way different schools either focused on different things and/or why they shared concern about common factors, while interpreting them differently. This paves the way for an understanding of how and why polemics became central to the way the tradition subsequently flourished. We shall see the purpose of the polemics, the points of controversy and dispute, the establishing of methodological criteria, and the importance to each tradition of arguing its case.

The following discussion presents a broadly chronological ordering of the ideas represented, so that developments can be understood in their context. The earliest traditions and schools of thought discussed in some detail are the Vedic sacrificial religion and the ideas and practices recorded in the early Upaniṣads. Not only do these represent the twin 'arms', so to speak, of the religion of the brahmin priests of ancient India, but they also provide the primary source material for several subsequent philosophical schools of thought, as well as the ground on which was based the need to establish the fundamentals of philosophical debate. Furthermore, it was against the hegemonic orthodoxy that this tradition established very early on that others reacted, putting forward counter-ideas and teachings. Notable among the latter was the Buddha, who lived for 80 years during the 5th century BCE. Because there is little Buddhism in India today, and nor was there at the time when the religious traditions of India were labelled 'Hinduism', the role of Buddhism in the Indian religio-philosophical tradition as a whole is often not appreciated. For more than a thousand years after the lifetime of the Buddha, Buddhism thrived in India, and from the beginning it played an enormously important and influential part in the challenging of the views of others and the flowering of different ideas. It in turn was strongly criticized by others. Chapters are devoted both to the early period of Buddhism and the way Buddhist ideas were first put forward, and to the more scholastically and/or philosophically systematic developments in Buddhist thought that emerged over the following centuries.

Over time, several schools of thought whose origins and associations are directly related in one way or another with the Vedic-Upaniṣadic tradition of the brahmins became recognizably systematized. Six gained prominence and have come to be called the six classical darśanas of India. Often they are called the six 'Hindu' darśanas, and while the label 'Hindu' is anachronistic and will not be used in this book, it does serve to distinguish them from Buddhist and other traditions, such as Jainism, which do not share the same direct lineage. What makes Buddhism and Jainism separate traditions in their own right was their outright and total rejection of the authority and teachings of the brahmins and the claims the brahmins made regarding the status of their primary sources. In contrast, the propounders of the six classical darśanas, while

Ontology

Ontology is concerned with being: it is about what there is. This can be a response on any scale from the microscopic to the cosmic to the question What is there? However one approaches ontological (what is there?) issues, the point is to ascertain the 'status of being' of what there is. This is called 'ontological status'. If one considers, say, a park as experienced in a dream and the supermarket where one does one's shopping, one can readily see that these two have different statuses of being – their ontological status is different. Similarly, an oasis seen in a mirage is of a different ontological status from an oasis one can locate by means of a map reference. Whatever there is has an ontological status. This need not be immediately obvious: during the dream or experience of the mirage, the park and the oasis seem to have the same status as the supermarket or map-referenced oasis. But in fact their status is different, and this difference can be understood in terms of reality. The supermarket is 'more real' than the dream park; the map-referenced oasis is 'more real' than the mirage. But the dream park and mirage do also have some kind of reality or status: they are experienced 'as real', and it is only with hindsight that one realizes they are 'less real' than other experiences. In the context of a worldview or philosophical system, its ontology is what it says there really is – even if we cannot immediately discern it – independent of any possible mistaken interpretations on our part of the dream/mirage kind. Through the ages in East and West, many different ontologies have been put forward. Some state that what we see is what there really is; others that our normal waking state is analagous to a dream state, and what really exists is different from that.

they engaged in argument and debate, and produced teachings and viewpoints that sometimes differed wildly, accepted Brahmanical authority and so remained within that fold.

The six classical darśanas, each of which is discussed in this book, are called *Nyāya*, *Vaiśeṣika*, *Yoga*, *Sāṃkhya*, *Mīmāṃsā*, and *Vedānta*. Traditionally, the six are treated as three pairs, with each pair having compatible or similar key features: Nyāya and Vaiśeṣika share an ontology (see the box on page 16) supplied by the latter with which the method of the former is compatible; Yoga and Sāṃkhya to a large extent share an ontology, again with which the method of the former is compatible; and Mīmāṃsā and Vedānta share an exegetical approach to different parts of the same corpus of material, to which they both ascribe the same primary status. This book follows these traditional pairings, devoting separate chapters to each pair. Where chronologically appropriate, however, chapters will contain references to key stages in other traditions in order to maintain an understanding of the way different schools of thought developed by means of interacting with each other.

Chapter 2
The Brahmanical Beginnings
Sacrifice, cosmic speculation, oneness

The beginning of the 5th century BCE: this is where we will begin our discussion of Indian philosophical thought, by looking at the ideas and practices established in northern India by brahmin priests at that time. This is a good place to start for several reasons. First, the milieu of north India at this period was dominated by the Brahmanical tradition, and it remained the only tradition to secure a lasting hegemonic grip on the country's socio-religious structure. No matter how influential the ideas and practices of others became at certain times, it was the Brahmanical tradition that retained control of normative criteria. Second, by the beginning of the 5th century BCE, two clearly identifiable approaches coexisted within this tradition, and we know enough about both to be able to highlight their key features and concerns. Third, and perhaps most importantly for our purposes, from a discussion of these two approaches we can see how they jointly contributed to the subsequent proliferation of questioning, debate, and attempts to refute the ideas of others. In establishing these points, we shall also see the way in which the two approaches emerged from earlier stages of the tradition.

Sacrifice

The brahmins of the 5th century BCE were the descendants of people called the Aryans, who came from central Eurasia and settled in

Chronology

c.2000–1500 BCE: The Vedic sacrificial tradition, based on ritual actions, was brought into north-west India by the Aryans. This tradition was preserved and administered by brahmin priests.

c.800–500 BCE: The teachings recorded in the early Upaniṣads, in which knowledge is said to be of ultimate importance, were embraced by the Brahmanical tradition.

By 500 BCE: these two branches – ritual and gnostic – of the Brahmanical tradition coexisted.

north-west India many centuries earlier, bringing their practices and ideas with them. For a very long time they had a sacrificial, ritual-based religion, the sacred details of which were carefully memorized and preserved in ritual 'manuals'. As writing was as yet unknown to them, different lineages of brahmin priests, each of which contributed to the rituals, had responsibility for the oral preservation of the material relating to their particular ritual duties. They took this responsibility extremely seriously, because it was on accuracy that the efficacy of the sacrifice depended. Memorization techniques of various kinds were perfected, and from the evidence we now have it is thought likely that a very high degree of accuracy was achieved.

Though it is now regarded as a religious activity, the performance of the Vedic sacrificial rituals was largely for this-worldly ends. That is, the primary purpose of the sacrifice was the maintenance of the cosmos at its optimum level of status quo. The sacrifices were addressed to aspects of the natural order of the cosmos, such as sun, rain, lightning, wind, and so on, as well as abstract principles, such as contract and vow. Collectively, addressees of the sacrifice were referred to as *devas*. The

The sacrificial rituals of the Aryans were performed by specialized people (brahmin priests), on behalf of those who had both a right and a duty to employ them. The sacrifice took place in a specially prepared space, arranged around a central fire or fires. To the accompaniment of spoken, chanted, and muttered words and sounds, special implements were used to make an offering into a fire of substances such as cooked grains and oil. All aspects of the sacrifice, from the measurements of the space to what substance should be offered and which words used, were prescribed in the ritual manuals.

rationale of the exercise was that if man performed the sacrificial rituals correctly, the devas would reciprocate by performing their cosmic function in the most beneficent way. Thus cosmic order – which later came to be known as *Dharma* – was maintained. The necessity to do this was enjoined upon the brahmins by the ritual manuals. These form the earliest parts of the corpus of material known as the Veda, so they can be referred to as the Vedic ritual manuals, and the sacrificial religion is sometimes referred to as the Vedic sacrificial religion.

The word *veda* means 'knowledge'. It refers to the belief that ancient ancestors of the 5th-century BCE brahmin priests knew or 'saw' the truth the Vedas contain (which is why they were called seers). This is understood not at all in terms of revealed, teacher-specific truth, but as impersonal and eternal cosmic truth, not of human origin, that the seers were merely instrumental in recording for posterity. As such, the status of the Vedic sacrificial texts is primary. And anything enjoined on man by this corpus of material is considered self-validating – it must be done because it must be done: this is part of eternal truth. The concern with accuracy to ensure efficacy was thus reinforced by the belief that the correct performance of each ritual act was part of cosmic duty.

1. Ritual implements used in Vedic sacrifice.

2. Vedic sacrificial rituals are still performed today, little changed from ancient times.

As well as physical ritual actions, the ritual manuals prescribed a variety of words and sounds, which can be referred to collectively as formulas, that had to be spoken, muttered, or chanted at the sacrifice. Both physical act and sound contributed to the results of the sacrifice: both were consequential 'actions', or karma. The language in which formulas were constructed was Sanskrit, and as a result the language was regarded more as a highly potent sacred tool than as a means of communication. It was seen, in effect, as the representation in sound form of the manifestation of the universe.

The language of Sanskrit

The word *saṃskṛt* shares a verbal root, *kṛ*, with the word karma. The prefix *saṃs* gives the word the meaning 'well-formed' or 'well-constructed'. This suggests the correlation between the correct sounding of Sanskrit words and the manifest universe to which they refer.

Because of the status and power of the Vedic material and the Sanskrit language, knowledge of both was closely guarded by the brahmin priests. They may have sought to legitimate this exclusivity on the grounds that such material needed protection, but at the same time it put the priests themselves in a position of supreme authority in the society of the time, and society itself was ordered in such a way as to maintain this authority. The origins of what is now called the caste system of India are recorded in the Vedic ritual manuals, where people are classified according to a hierarchy of ritual purity, with the brahmins, the purest, at the top. Their purity both entitled and enabled them to associate safely and effectively with the sacred actions and language of the sacrifice.

So the main characteristics of the Vedic sacrificial religion were that it was based on ritual actions, both physical and verbal, the precise

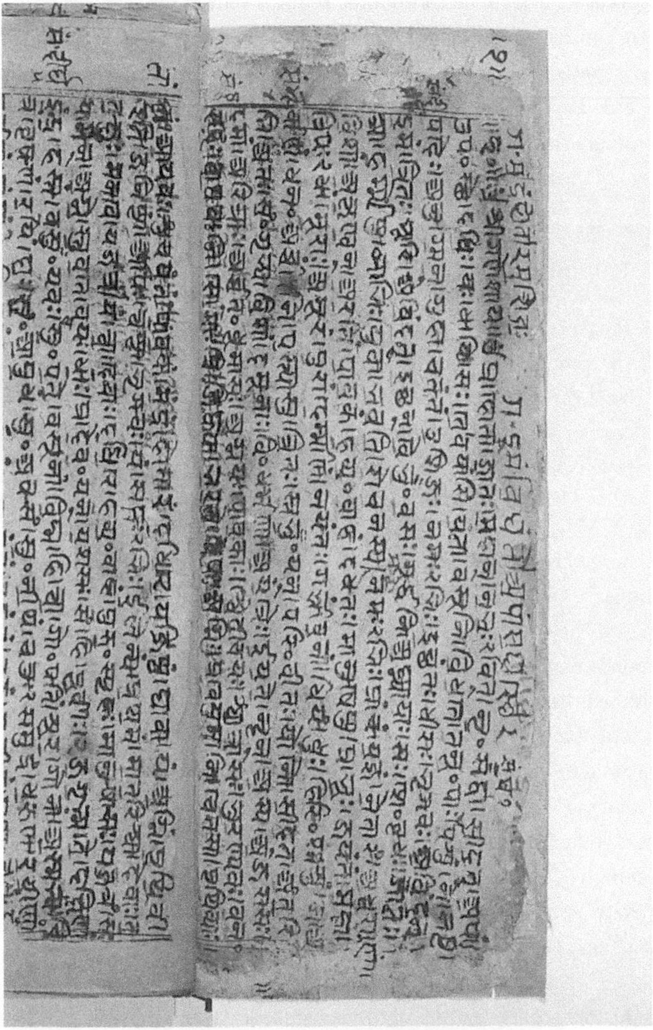

3. Extract from the *Ṛg Veda*, manuscript dated 1434 AD.

accuracy of which was essential to ensure efficacy, and it was wholly preserved and administered by brahmin priests. The purpose of the performance of ritual practices was the maintenance of cosmic continuity, and the various actions of the sacrifice – physical and verbal – were believed to be correlated with their effects accordingly.

Cosmic Speculation

This-worldy though the system largely was, many of the Vedic texts record that some of the ancient ritual specialists were also sophisticated speculators about the nature of the cosmos they sought to sustain. They realized that the parts played by the devas to whom the sacrifices were addressed were limited to the particular place and role each had in the cosmos, and they speculated as to whether there might be something greater. They also wanted to know more about the origins of the cosmos itself. How did it all begin? Who or what (if anyone or anything) created it? Did it begin as a golden embryo? Was it constructed by a heavenly architect? Did it emerge out of a cosmic sacrifice? What role did speech play (that is, the sound of the sacred language)? Was breath the animator of all things? Or was it time that began it all? What was there before? and perhaps most important: Who knows about it?

This ancient speculation is extraordinary in its extent and profundity, and suggests a considerable degree of analytical thinking on the part of the ritualists about the nature of what it was they were doing. We have no evidence that the speculation affected the rituals themselves; indeed, it would be unlikely that it did because the rituals were so precisely codified. But it is possible that ongoing questioning contributed to a second strand of ideas and religious practice being embraced by the Brahmanical tradition. Alongside the continuing practice by the majority of outward and visible sacrificial rituals, the Vedic texts record that some began to go on retreat to contemplate the nature of the sacrifice in more depth. Eventually, some of these people

There was neither non-existence nor existence then; there was neither the realm of space nor the sky which is beyond. What stirred? Where? In whose protection? Was there water, bottomlessly deep?

There was neither death nor immortality then. There was no distinguishing sign of night nor of day. That one breathed, windless, by its own impulse. Other than that there was nothing beyond.

Darkness was hidden by darkness in the beginning; with no distinguishing sign, all this was water. The life force that was covered with emptiness, that one arose through the power of heat. . . .

Who really knows? Who will here proclaim it? Whence was it produced? Whence is this creation? The devas came afterwards, with the creation of this universe. Who then knows whence it has arisen?

Whence this creation has arisen – perhaps it formed itself, or perhaps it did not – the one who looks down on it, in the highest heaven, only he knows – or perhaps he does not know.

(*Ṛg Veda* 10.129, from *The Rig Veda: An Anthology*, ed. and trans. by Wendy Doniger O'Flaherty, Harmondsworth: Penguin, 1981)

The dating of the *Ṛg Veda* is uncertain, but is thought to be considerably earlier than the 5th century BCE – possibly as early as 1500 BCE.

came to think that the sacrifice could be 'internalized', practised by means of concentration and visualization techniques.

The gradual development of this trend is recorded in books of the Vedic corpus of material known as Brāhmaṇas and Āraṇyakas (see the box below), but it is in the Upaniṣads that teachings are found which might specifically represent its culmination. The Upaniṣads form the final part of the Vedic canon – they are called the 'end of the Veda' – and their contents were gathered in the same Brahmanical lineages as the ritual material.

The Vedic material was preserved in different Brahmanical lineages. Four 'strands' of **ritual manual**, used by different kinds of brahmin priests, were supplemented over time by **Brāhmaṇas**, **Āraṇyakas**, and finally, **Upaniṣads**:

The four ritual strands were:

Ṛg Veda	Sāma Veda	Yajur Veda	Atharva Veda

Into these lineages were incorporated **Brāhmaṇa** and **Āraṇyaka** texts, which contained ideas on the nature of the sacrifice and of 'internalizing the sacrifice'.

The **Upaniṣads** form appendices to the earlier material:

Kauśītaki	*Chāndogya*	*Taittirīya*	*Muṇḍaka*
	Kena	*Bṛhadāraṇyaka*	*Praśna*
		Kaṭha	
		Īśa	
		Śvetāśvatara	

The Upaniṣads contain a great deal, speculative and instructive, on the nature, purpose, and necessity of the performance of sacrificial rituals. But what distinguishes them from earlier Brahmanical texts is that they also contain teachings and ideas that subordinate the rationale of the ritual to an imperative to seek to understand the nature of the human being. Further, the knowledge that was sought was subjective and esoteric – inner, 'spiritual' knowledge – in contrast with the exoteric, ritual knowledge of the sacrifice. This marks a shift in the tradition from its previous cosmos-centred concerns to more person-centred issues – or rather it brings the individual person into more specific focus within the broader cosmic picture of the earlier purely ritual period. The early Upaniṣads contain the first known record of the idea that human beings are reborn again and again into circumstances conditioned by their actions in previous lives. They state that the dutiful and correct performance of sacrifices will not only bring about the consequences to which the sacrifices are addressed, but will also beneficially affect the conditions of one's next life. This is the law of karma (action) applied not just to ritual but also to the mechanics of human experience.

The most important thing to aspire to, however, is gaining insight into the nature of one's essential self or soul, called *ātman* in Sanskrit. The Upaniṣads teach that self and cosmos are one, repeatedly stating that one's ātman is inseparable from all that there is. This is famously expressed as *tat tvam asi*: 'you are [all] that' (*Chāndogya Upaniṣad* 6.8 ff). Gaining experiential insight of this identity is to be aspired to because such knowledge effects one's release (in Sanskrit, *mokṣa*) from continued rebirth. This teaching introduces the idea of salvation into the Brahmanical tradition for the first time, and while sacrificial rituals have continued to be practised to this day, the experience of mokṣa was quickly established as the supreme goal of human existence. It was seen in the wholly positive sense of knowledge which enabled one to escape from the treadmill of rebirth and experience immortality: 'One who sees this does not experience death, sickness, or distress [any more].' (*Chāndogya Upaniṣad* 7.26.2)

Oneness

Looked at from the point of view of the universal rather than the particular, the teaching that self and cosmos are identical also responds to earlier speculation as to the nature of the cosmos. In the early Upaniṣads, the universe is referred to by the neuter term *Brahman* (not to be confused with its masculine form, *Brahmā*, which is the name of an important deva in the tradition). Brahman is the equivalent of an impersonal absolute that might also be called Oneness or Being. An important passage, in which a father is instructing his son, states:

> In the beginning, this world was just Being - one only, without a second. It is true that some people say 'In the beginning this world was just non-existence - one only, without a second; and from that non-existence

> The teaching that the universe is One is referred to by the ontological term *monism*. This means that there is only one existent thing, and there is nothing that is not that thing. So whatever there is is ultimately the same thing, even if this does not appear to us to be the case: we do not have to be able to see it for it to be true. Monism is a numerical, not a qualitative, term. Other information is required in order to know the nature and characteristics, if any, of the oneness.
>
> Monism is not a theistic term either, and should not be confused with *monotheism*. Monotheism states that there is one God, but tells us nothing else about what there is per se. It is not stating there is only oneness. If the universe is monistic, within that oneness it is possible that there might be thought to be something that appears as God - or, indeed, many gods - but this would have no more bearing on the underlying oneness than the apparent plurality of the empirical world does.

Being emerged.' But how could that possibly be the case? How could Being come from non-existence? On the contrary, in the beginning, this world was just Being – one only, without a second.'

(*Chāndogya Upaniṣad* 6.2.1–2)

The early Upaniṣads are full of statements drawing out the implications of such oneness: 'It is by seeing, hearing, reflecting, and concentrating on one's essential self (ātman) that the whole world is known.' (*Bṛhadāraṇyaka Upaniṣad* 2.4.5). 'The ātman is below, above, to the west, east, south, and north; the ātman is, indeed, the whole world.' (*Chāndogya Upaniṣad* 7.25.2). Mostly straightforwardly, the expression 'ātman is Brahman' unequivocally identifies essential self with cosmos, ultimately not two things but one.

The focus on the identity of inner self and cosmos suggests that the teachings contained in the Upaniṣads might be seen as the culmination of the internalization of the sacrifice, as suggested above. The outward and visible practices directed towards the external world are simply transposed to an inner understanding of the world. The Upaniṣads also uphold the tradition of the sacrificial ritual in that at no point do they suggest that rituals should be abandoned. On the contrary, they reinforce both the need to perform rituals and the hierarchical social structure, based on ritual purity, within which they operate. Thus it was that both ritual and Upaniṣadic teachings could coexist alongside each other within the Brahmanical tradition. The primary status accorded to the Vedic ritual manuals is similarly accorded to the Upaniṣads in that both are considered to contain teachings about the truth.

One can also immediately see, however, the way in which these two strands of the tradition embrace issues and views that are potentially divisive or internally contentious. Not only do the focus and emphasis shift in the Upaniṣads from the this-worldly concerns of the ritual to the nature and destiny of the person, as described above; it is also the case that the attaining of esoteric knowledge is considered of superior significance and purpose than the performing of ritual actions. Furthermore, and perhaps most importantly, the Vedic practice of rituals and the Upaniṣadic seeking of knowledge are each underpinned by a different understanding of the nature of reality. The Upaniṣads make it clear that rituals, while important, are merely what should take place within a worldview which assumes the transcendental reality of the plural world: indeed, the purpose of the rituals is to maintain that plural world. But such plurality, the Upaniṣads suggest, is only empirically (or conventionally) real, and it is knowledge of the greater reality of the underlying oneness of the world that leads to the higher goal of immortality:

> 'There is really no diversity here. He goes from death to death who perceives diversity here. One must see it as just one . . . by knowing that very one, a wise brahmin can obtain insight for himself.'
>
> (*Bṛhadāraṇyaka Upaniṣad* 4.4.19)

Those who state that the plurality of the world around us is ultimately real are *pluralists*. Other terms for this ontology are *pluralistic realism* and *transcendental realism*. This means that what we see – the plurality of the empirical world – is real in itself, transcendent (or 'outside') of anything to do with human perception.

Those who state that empirical plurality is not transcendentally real (and this would include those who state that reality is one) are not denying empirical reality. Rather, what they are stating is that there is a greater degree of reality – absolute reality – that differs from what we see on the surface. Empirical reality in this case is 'conventional'.

In the early decades of the 5th century BCE, these two approaches do not appear to have been mutually contentious or to have given rise to incompatible worldviews vying for supremacy. But as we shall see in following chapters, this soon changed. Not only did this century see the Buddha and others challenge Brahmanical teachings based on the Upaniṣads, but it soon became necessary for ritual specialists to defend their realistic worldview against those who sought to refute or ridicule the point of the sacrifice. And in doing so they themselves had to refute any notion of the merely conventional status of the empirical world such as suggested in the Upaniṣads, as well as by others. This meant that not only did the Brahmanical tradition have to grapple with criticism from outside, but it also became increasingly exposed to internal divergence based on its two branches of primary material.

Later, some who were concerned not to question the legitimacy of the presence of both approaches within the same tradition sought to overcome their incompatibility by suggesting that ritual duties should be carried out during the period of one's life when one was married and producing children. This would mean both that the maintenance of the ritual-dependent world would be ensured, and also that succeeding generations of sons, on whom the continuity of the brahmin-led social hierarchy depended, would be produced. Once this stage of life had passed, attention could then be focused on the quest for liberating knowledge. To this day, those whose primary concern is religious practice rather than philosophical debate see this as the path of Brahmanical orthodoxy that acknowledges the primary status of the whole of the Veda.

As the more philosophical and polemical debate developed, thinkers from a variety of traditions became involved, but in the direct lineage of this early material, two of the classical darśanas – Mīmāṃsā and Vedānta – based their different teachings and worldviews on exegesis of the Vedic ritual material and the Upaniṣads respectively. These two bodies of material, on which were based the ritual and gnostic branches of the Brahmanical tradition that coexisted during the early part of the 5th century BCE, came to be known by challengers, reconcilers, and exegetes alike as the 'action section' (*karma-kāṇḍa*) and the 'knowledge section' (*jñāna-kāṇḍa*) of the Veda.

Chapter 3
Renouncing the Household

The Buddha's Middle Way

Renouncer v. Householder

The correlation between religious power and social hierarchy, administered and guarded by the brahmins with the same degree of rigidity as the sacrificial ritual itself, was such that some found the prospect of living within the strictures of the Brahmanical fold oppressive. Such people sought alternative socio-religious paths, and collectively became known as renouncers (*śramaṇa*). What they rejected was everything to do with the authority and prescriptive norms of the brahmin priests, but 'renouncer' tends to be understood more specifically as the polar opposite of the 'householder' status prescribed by the Brahmanical tradition in order to ensure its continuity. Householders had a duty not just to sacrifice but also to be economically productive and sexually reproductive, within group lineages which excluded those not of the same status of ritual purity. Renouncers, in contrast, tended to be peripatetic, mendicant, and celibate. Some grouped round leaders whose teachings and insights they accepted and agreed with, but many were solitary wanderers. Many also practised severe austerities, subjecting themselves to extremes of temperature, hunger and thirst, painful bodily distortions, and various other kinds of self-denial. Such asceticism was believed by renouncers to be purposeful in that it was thought to contribute to gaining spiritual insight by focusing the mind in certain non-normative ways.

Chronology

c.*2000* BCE– : the Vedic sacrificial tradition.

c.*800–500* BCE: the early Upaniṣads.

by 500 BCE: ritual and gnostic branches of the Brahmanical tradition coexisted.

5th-century BCE *milieu*: in polar contrast to the householders of the Brahmanical religion were the renouncers – peripatetic, mendicant, and celibate wanderers, in search of knowledge about the world and the self. Renouncers rejected all Brahmanical norms.

c.*485–405* BCE: the lifetime of the Buddha. Texts record that the Buddha challenged Brahmanical practices and teachings, and their claims to authority, and found no satisfactory alternative among the teachings of the renouncers. Based on insights gained at his own Enlightenment, he taught a Middle Way between those of the householders and the renouncers.

We do not know exactly how or when renouncers became a significant presence in the milieu of north India in which the worldview of the brahmins was becoming dominant in the period before the 5th century BCE. During the 20th century, excavations of a previously unknown, extremely ancient civilization in the Indus Valley produced evidence which suggested that there had been a very early indigenous tradition, thriving long before the Aryans arrived, that the renouncers might have been the inheritors of: that is, the approach and practices of the renouncers might not have originated within the Aryan tradition. Whatever the source, it nevertheless might have been the

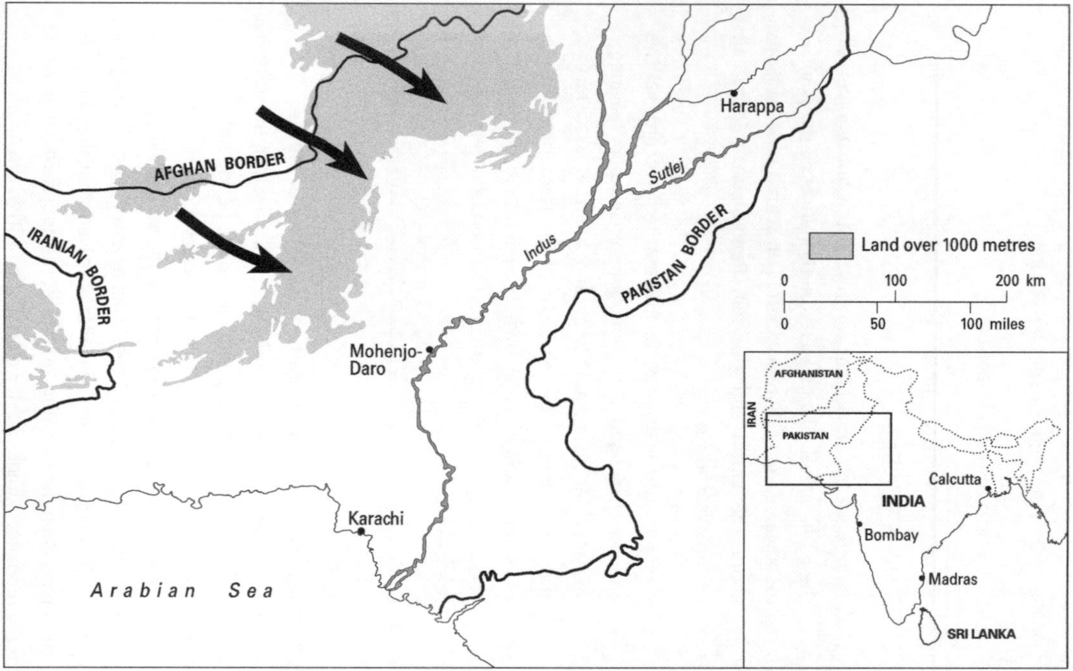

Map 1. Map showing the two main city centres of the Indus Valley Civilization, Mohenjo-Daro and Harappa.

4. A view of Mohenjo-daro.

case that as some of those within the brahmin fold sought to internalize the purpose and practice of sacrificial rituals, they also sought to bypass the strictures of priestly involvement within a prescribed social structure. It is also possible that the trend to internalize the sacrifice might itself have been triggered by contact with indigenous practices.

What we do know, from various sources that corroborate one another, is that, by the time the Brahmanical tradition was embracing the new teachings recorded in the Upaniṣads, there was a significant number of peripatetic renouncers who were seeking their own answers to religio-philosophical questions. In many respects, the questions themselves related to the same issues as those addressed both in Vedic speculative material and in the Upaniṣads. That is to say, it was not that the renouncers were seeking truth of a wholly different kind, only that they sought answers by their own means rather than as taught by the brahmins. The concern of virtually all of them was to understand the nature of the world and the nature of the human being, expressed in terms of selfhood.

The Nature of Self

Our sources suggest there was a wide variety of theories relating to the nature of self and world, the emphasis on either or both varying with each point of view. The plethora of questions on selfhood is summed up in an early Buddhist text as follows:

> Did I exist in the past? Did I not exist in the past? What was I in the past? How was I in the past? Having been what, what did I become in the past? Shall I exist in the future? How shall I be in the future? Having been what, what shall I become in the future? Am I now? Am I not, now? What am I? How am I? Where has this being come from? Where will this being go?

It goes on to give putative answers:

'I have a self. I have no self. I perceive [my] self by means of [my] self. I perceive no self by means of [my] self. I perceive [my] self by means of no self. This self of mine which speaks and feels, that experiences the consequences of good and bad actions now here and now there, this self is permanent, stable, eternal, unchanging, the same always.'

(*Majjhima Nikāya* I 8)

So numerous were the speculative questions on both self and world that all possibilities came to be subsumed in a formula in Buddhist texts:

Is the world eternal or not? Is the world finite or not? Is the self different from the body or not? On achieving liberation from rebirth, does one exist or not exist, exist and not exist, neither exist nor not exist?

(*Saṃyutta Nikāya* II 223, for example – paraphrase)

From this and other generalizing evidence can be drawn certain broad streams of thought. Some held to a strongly materialist view, proclaiming the radical physicality of human beings in a wholly finite and temporally limited world. Others stated that while there might be some kind of immaterial self associated with one's physical body during one's lifetime, it ceases once and for all at death. People who held this view were referred to as annihilationists in early Buddhist sources: death involves the 'annihilation' of the self. Neither annihilationists nor strong materialists saw any point in taking seriously the idea that a law of karma operated for human beings. But many, possibly most, of the renouncers contextualized their views within a framework which posited human beings experiencing a series of lives. Some, along with the Upaniṣadic brahmins, held that the self is permanent and unchanging, and were called eternalists by Buddhists. Others were not eternalistic, but did believe in some kind of continuity. All such people believed that actions have consequences for future lives, and for them the whole point of seeking answers to these questions was that this particular knowledge – knowledge of the nature of the self and its ontological context – was believed to effect liberation (mokṣa) from rebirth. It was for this reason that their search for answers was so crucial, and that it was on questions relating to these issues that their attention remained focused.

This is an important point to grasp, as it represents a key characteristic of the milieu we are attempting to understand. To draw it out more clearly, it might help if we consider the picture from a slightly different angle. What we have, broadly speaking, is a milieu in which one can see that different practices and concerns are directly correlated with respectively appropriate worldviews.

On the one hand there were those following the ancient Brahmanical tradition of the Vedic sacrificial religion, in which the performing of rituals was directly linked to the maintaining of a universe which, if not entirely empirical, was certainly plural and real. Concern centred on the precision of the sacrifice because of the link between act and effect. This ancient tradition was at this time on the verge of being overshadowed by other approaches, represented by the teachings of the Upaniṣads and the concerns of the non-materialist renouncers. But it had already become the standard-bearer of orthodoxy, establishing social norms which endure to the modern day. Its presence and influence were thus not going to be brushed aside no matter how strongly alternative approaches claimed superiority.

Others, such as materialists and annihilationists, held to a worldview which precluded focusing on anything other than the here and now. These people concerned themselves primarily with defending their standpoint and attempting to refute what they saw as the absurd claims and practices of both ritualists and non-materialists alike.

At the other end of the spectrum were those who thought life was a karmically determined round of rebirths and the world something other or more than its empirical appearance. Their concern was with gaining knowledge of the precise structure of the world as it is in reality and the place of human beings within it. This not only enabled them to make lofty claims of knowledge of metaphysical truth, but also gave them the existential imperative to realize the means of effecting release from bondage to rebirth. If they wished to attain this highest of prizes, what they had to know about above all else was the nature of the self. This quest thus dominated their approach, effectively excluding any other concerns or issues.

Gotama – the Buddha

This is the milieu into which was born, around 485 BCE, a man named Siddhartha Gotama, later to become known as the Buddha. The word *buddha* literally means 'awake', and alludes to the occasion of the Buddha's Enlightenment. This is described in texts as the attaining of insight (or rather three insights), the nature of which was significant enough to be understood as analogous to waking up after having been asleep. This point draws attention to the structure of the Buddhist path, which, in common with that taught by the Upaniṣadic brahmins and many of the renouncers, is to progress from ignorance to knowledge. Ignorance is the prime conditioning factor in fuelling ongoing rebirth, with each life characterized by the profound unsatisfactorinesses associated with the transience of everything one can experience. Knowledge is the enabling factor in bringing about the cessation of this continuous rebirth. It was because the early teachers in these traditions claimed to have gained access to such knowledge that we have such an abundance of different metaphysical theories from this period.

Notwithstanding the free circulation of many popular stories, based on the Buddhist tradition's didactic and hagiographic narrative literature, we have no certain facts regarding the Buddha's early life, except that he was born into a family who lived in the town of Kapilavatthu (in what is now Nepal) and that it seems likely that the family was well-to-do with high connections. The texts recount that he left home in his early 30s in order to seek an answer to questions concerning the existential nature of the human lot: Why is human existence as it is? Why is it characterized by disease, ageing, and death? Is it inevitable that it is like this? Can one do anything about it? Can one, indeed, escape such an existence?

Whether or not the Buddha had any knowledge of any of the teachings recounted above prior to leaving home (we do not know either way), the earliest Buddhist texts tell us that once he set out on his quest he encountered people with a very wide range of views. Indeed, these texts are one of our most important sources of information, alongside early Jain texts, about the range of views in the milieu. Searching as he was for answers to big questions, the Buddha was actively interested in encountering others on similar quests and in learning what they thought was relevant to the situation and what one might do about it. It seems that he spent some years listening to, learning, and testing their theories by following their example in various kinds of practices. He did not feel that any of them provided the certain answers he was in search of, and eventually he decided to try his own technique in an attempt to gain the deeper insights he sought.

Using a penetrative form of meditation he was later to teach, the Buddha claimed he had gained three insights, which together gave him understanding of how and why human existence is as it is. He also claimed that he had, through these insights, achieved release from bondage to its continuity. First, he was able to see his previous lives, and the way in which each had influenced the quality and conditions of subsequent lives: that is, he could see his own rebirth history. Second, he saw the way other beings were born and reborn, again according to the conditioning effects of actions in previous lives. The Buddha's acceptance and teaching of rebirth and karma were thus not based on his adoption of features of a prevailing worldview: rather, they were

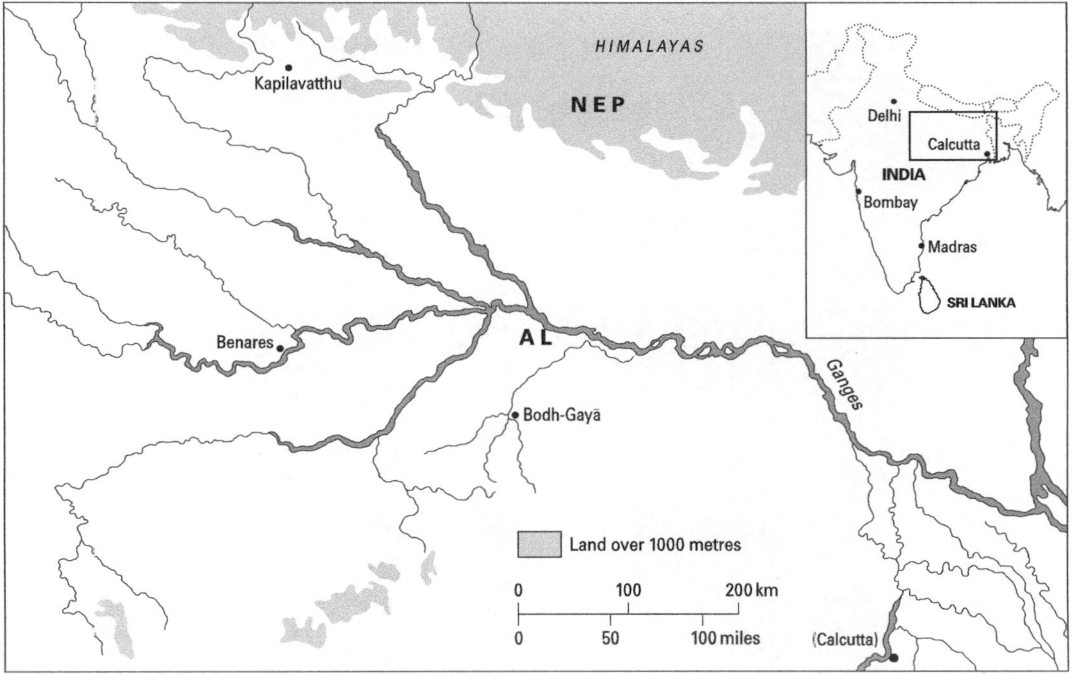

Map 2. Sites associated with the Buddha.

5. A Buddhist monk meditates.

based on his own experience. The third insight was how to uproot from his psycho-conceptual framework those factors which he could see most deeply bound him to worldly continuity: appetitive desires, the desire for continued existence, ignorance of the true nature of reality, and the holding of opinionated 'views'.

The Buddha's Enlightenment

'With my mind concentrated, clarified, purified, free from interferences, supple, and focused, I directed my mind towards knowing how to uproot the 'continuity tendencies'. I could see as it really is the primary characteristic of human existence, how it arises, that it can cease, and the way leading to its cessation. I knew as they really are the continuity tendencies, their arising, their ceasing, and how to achieve their cessation. Knowing and seeing thus, my mind achieved freedom from the binding effects of all appetitive desires, my mind achieved freedom from the binding effects of desiring continued becoming, my mind achieved freedom from the binding effects of holding to opinionated views, and my mind achieved freedom from the binding effects of ignorance. I then knew for certain that I was liberated from rebirth, I had practised what was necessary, done what had to be done, and my present state would generate no further continuity.'

(*Vinaya* III 4 – paraphrase)

(See also *Majjhima Nikāya* I 23 and *Aṅguttara Nikāya* II 211 and IV 179.)

According to the texts (see the box above), prior to describing the third insight the Buddha summed up what he could see in a fourfold formula: (1) human existence is intrinsically characterized in a certain way; (2) specific factors fuel its continuity; (3) cessation of that continuity is possible; (4) there is a way leading to cessation. Seeing and

6. Image of the Buddha teaching.

understanding the key aspects of this situation is what is necessary if what one is seeking is to gain liberation from bondage to it. So fundamental was this that it became his first actual teaching to others, known as the Four Noble Truths, said to have been given in a deer park in Varanasi.

The Four Noble Truths

The structure of the Four Noble Truths is simple and clear: X is the case because of Y, and will cease if Y ceases, where X is intrinsic to human existence. What they refer to in conceptual terms is less easy to draw out, partly because of their cryptic nature and partly because *dukkha*, the Pāli term used to refer to the intrinsic characteristic of human existence identified in the first Noble Truth, is far from clear in its meaning. Dukkha has often been translated as 'suffering', 'pain', or 'ill', but it is now widely recognized that this wrongly attributes to the Buddha a deeply negative, and readily refutable, view of human existence. A better translation is 'unsatisfactoriness', which conceptually relates dukkha to the Buddha's teaching that all of the factors of our phenomenal world of existence are impermanent. In direct contrast to the claims of the Upaniṣadic teachers of his day – that in spite of apparent pluralities the universe is in fact a permanent and unchanging essential oneness that it was possible to gain insight of – the Buddha taught that all of the factors of experience were impermanent. And because they are impermanent, they are ultimately unsatisfactory (even the best of experiences and situations do not last) in contrast to the assumed blissfulness of immortality, or essential permanence. Thus the Four Noble Truths are understood to identify this unsatisfactoriness-based-on-transience as the fundamental characteristic of cyclical life. It is because one does not accept impermanence, and constantly seeks and desires that things be permanent – youth, healthiness, loved ones, treasured possessions, and so on – that one fuels the continuity of unsatisfactoriness, as one's very desires are doomed to disappointment. In reiteration of the second

The Buddha's Teachings

The Four Noble Truths

Human existence is intrinsically characterized by dukkha.
Dukkha arises because of appetitive cravings and desires (negative and positive).
There can be a cessation of dukkha, known as *nirvana*.
Nirvana is achieved by following the Noble Eightfold Path.

(*Saṃyutta Nikāya* V 420, for example – paraphrase)

Nirvana means 'blowing out', and refers to the cessation of the fuel of continuity.

Dependent Origination

'What I teach is dependent origination, that all knowable things are dependently originated; this is the way things are, the regularity of things.'

(*Saṃyutta Nikāya* II 25)

When this is, that is;
This occurring, that occurs;
When this is not, that is not;
This ceasing, that ceases.

(*Majjhima Nikāya* III 63, for example)

The Three Marks of Existence

All conditioned things are impermanent.
All conditioned things are [therefore] unsatisfactory.
All knowable things are not-self.

(*Dhammapada* 277–9, for example)

> The formulaic form in which key teachings of early Buddhism have come down to us reflects the fact that until they were written down in approximately 40 BCE, the early guardians of the tradition used mnemonic devices in order to preserve them orally.

Noble Truth, Buddhism teaches that this is where the mechanism of the karmic process lies: in one's appetitive cravings and desires, one's intentional state of mind.

The reason one continues to desire and crave what cannot be attained is because one is ignorant of the true nature of reality. In reality, everything within the cycle of lives is conditioned by something else. The Buddha made this point in another of his key teachings. There is, he stated, a 'way things are', a 'regularity of things', which is that all things are 'dependently originated'. This is generic to all of the factors of our cyclical experience: nothing at all, of whatever nature – material or mental, sensory or conceptual, concrete or abstract, organic or inorganic – occurs independently of conditioning factors. Indeed, this is the reason for the impermanence of all things.

Dependent Origination

Dependent origination is a profoundly radical metaphysical teaching. It is not stating that nothing exists, but that the manner in which all things occur is different from either existence, which implies independence, or non-existence, which implies a denial of occurrence. The point of the Buddha's teaching on dependent origination is that it takes the 'middle way' between existence, non-existence, existence-and-non-existence, and neither-existence-nor-non-existence. This logic-defying formula, which we have already seen above, is designed to include and reject all possible permutations of metaphysical positions taken by others.

The Buddha's 'Middle Way'

The Buddha said that what he taught took a middle way between the teachings and practices of the householders and the renouncers. This can most clearly be seen in three areas:

1 The Buddhist monastic community functioned in a manner between the extremes of fully upholding the social structure and wholly rejecting it: members lived apart from society, but were interdependent with the laity.

2 The monastic Buddhist's daily regime and way of life were between the sensory indulgence associated with family life and the severe self-inflicted austerities endured by the renouncers: they were celibate, but all other needs were met in order to maintain the healthy well-being thought important for full commitment to the path.

3 The metaphysics of dependent origination took a middle way between all possible permutations of the ontological theories offered by others: it could not be expressed in any combination of terms relating to existence or non-existence.

It is frequently stated that what the Buddha was teaching in this context, in direct contrast to the Upaniṣadic brahmins and others, was that there is no self. This view arises from the use of the Pāli term *anattā* (Sanskrit *anātman*), which involves the attaching of a negative prefix to the word for 'self'. Selfhood, as we have seen, was of central concern to most others in the Buddha's milieu. The dominant Brahmanical group, teaching from the Upaniṣads, were claiming that knowledge of the self's immortal identity with the essence of the universe brought liberation. The Buddha, in contrast, stated that all knowable things (*dhammā*) are anattā, 'not-self'. And Buddhists and scholars alike have taken this as a radical denial of selfhood: no self exists.

Recent scholarship has pointed out, however, that the context is one of generic, and not just subjective, applicability. The point is that if all things are dependently originated, between all permutations of existence and non-existence, then the manner in which all things occur – including selves in the same way as musical notes, toenails, thoughts, laughter, aromas, cats, trees, chairs, and stones – is generically the same, not that they are non-existent. Indeed, non-existence is specifically denied. Because of its subjective connotations, the term anattā can act as a red herring. The Buddha was denying not people's selves, but that anything exists independently. This clearly is in contrast to the claims of others of the permanence of selfhood, but that it is stating that there is no self is questionable.

Its questionability is supported by the fact that the Buddha urged that one should refrain from taking any such ontological position with regard to the self or of the world. He stated that all and any of these were 'mere opinions' – contributing to the most deeply binding continuity factors needing to be uprooted on gaining insight into the nature of reality. He himself refused to answer questions on such issues, and his silence when questioned on the 'fourfold logic' formula referred to above gave rise to their appellation as the Unanswered Questions of Buddhism. In great contrast both to his contemporaries and to most other teachers, no information on the ontological status of self and world is given by the Buddha – or at least not directly. What the Buddha does teach – in order to 'see things as they really are', as it is put in Buddhist sources – is that the focus of one's investigation and understanding should not be ontological issues, but the operation of one's cognitive faculties.

These are referred to in Buddhist sources as a fivefold interacting apparatus, called the five *khandhas*, a word which has no exact English equivalent in this context. If an interlocutor appears to be directing attention elsewhere, the Buddha frequently reiterates that it is the operating of the khandhas that needs to be understood. Furthermore, and most importantly, it is repeatedly stated in the early texts that the five khandhas are what constitute dukkha, the primary characteristic of human existence identified in the first Noble Truth. This association suggests that the full import of the Truth is, therefore, not confined to the psychological state of unsatisfactoriness, but includes the point that where an investigation of human existence must start is with one's cognitive apparatus. This is the means whereby one has any experience at all, and thus nothing specific can be investigated or known about without first understanding the means by which one experiences it, or has any notion of it in the first place.

In 'religious' terms, the purpose of the investigation of one's cognitive apparatus is to understand the link between the way it normally operates and the way one's cravings and desires affect it: appetitive response is dependent on cognitive processes that operate normatively, but in fact, according to the true nature of reality, erroneously. In particular, the failure to understand the implications of dependent origination lead one to continue to respond as an independent desirer, having individual desires for separate objects of desire. In this way is continuity fuelled by a combination of ignorance and appetitive cravings. Conversely, the appetitive cravings will atrophy if and when ignorance is replaced by understanding that the perception of independence and separateness is false.

From the Nature of Being to the Nature of Experience

From the 'philosophical' point of view, what this teaching does is to shift the focus of investigation from ontology to epistemology. That is to say, into the milieu of intense metaphysical questioning and ontological theories relating to the self and the world, the Buddha interjects the claim that all one has access to is one's own subjective cognitive process. One cannot get outside of this to see or check what might be the case external to it, but one can nevertheless understand how it works. This involves understanding how it is involved in the structuring of the way we experience the world about us. The texts make reference to the way one's perceiving apparatus processes the 'raw' data of experience into increasingly identifiable, refined, and sophisticated categories, the whole process involving 'making manifold what is not really manifold' (*Aṅguttara Nikāya* II 161).

The cognitive process

> Visual sensation occurs when there is contact between consciousness, eye, and visual object; that preliminary sensation is then identified, conceptualized, and made manifold.
>
> (*Majjhima Nikāya* I 111 – paraphrase)

This pattern is identical for hearing, smelling, tasting, touching or thinking (six senses, including one relating to non-sensory mental activity, are recognized in Buddhism and other Indian schools of thought).

Dependent origination again

> 'Understanding dependent origination means one *will no longer ask* questions about the existence of the self, past, future, or present, such as Is it? or Is it not?, What is it?, Why is it?, this Thing that it is – Where has it come from? Where will it go?'
>
> (*Saṃyutta Nikāya* IV 93 – paraphrase, my italics)

Two implications arise from this teaching that are not made explicit in the texts (indeed, little is made explicit). One is that if it is one's perceiving apparatus that processes all experiential data, then this is what forms the matrix of dependent origination: whatever one experiences is dependently originated in subjective experiencing processes. This means not only that there is a direct correlation between subjectivity and objectivity, but also that what makes the dependently originated phenomena of cyclical existence impermanent is their experiential nature. This implication was to become more fully drawn out and discussed in later Buddhism, particularly in Yogācāra Buddhism, but in the early period largely remained latent.

The other is that if the focus lies in understanding the nature of knowing as opposed to the nature of things, as it were, independent of our knowing faculties, then it follows that nothing one knows is one's self. Whatever might be its nature or ontological status, a knowing subject cannot objectify itself in order to be known by itself. Thus one reads in the last line of a formula known as the Three Characteristics of Existence (shown in the box on p. 48): 'All knowable things (*dhammā*) are not-self (anattā)'. This implication has also largely remained latent, in this case because of contrasting claims that the anattā doctrine is stating that there is no self.

The Buddha was a harsh critic of the views and claims of others in many respects. If his anattā teaching was stating there is no self, this alone would be in radical contrast to the claims of at least the dominant Brahmanical group, teaching from the Upaniṣads. If, in fact, its purport was that nothing one can know is one's self, then he would most profoundly have undercut not just the teaching of the dominant Brahmanical group, but the very rationale of the quest as seen by the vast majority of his contemporaries. In any case, in teaching dependent origination he rejected outright all of the various ontological stances taken by others.

In drawing out the various features of what he taught, however, it is important to remember that at the time his purpose both in teaching, and in rejecting the teachings of others, was entirely directed towards helping others to gain insight in order to achieve liberation from the vicissitudes of human existence. One cannot read the early Buddhist texts without being constantly reminded of this motive, and to ignore or omit this point would be to do violence to the way the teachings are preserved. The Buddha was concerned to undermine the brahmins not because he wished to win a philosophical point but because he saw their claims to exclusivity and supreme authority as pernicious to people's well-being. Furthermore, he considered their dependence on tradition for how they claim things are, rather than drawing on their own individual experiential understanding, to be deeply unreliable, to the extent of being inherently self-invalidating: he saw no reason why anyone should believe a teaching given by someone who has never experienced what they are making claims about. He also objected to their self-importance and lack of concern for the liberation of others. He regarded all priestly ritual activity as purposeless: the action – consequence mechanism that mattered lay in one's state of mind, he said, and no one had access to that but oneself. He saw the focus on remembering sacred formulas precisely, and guarding a sacred language from others, as diverting attention away from the need to understand the structure of existential mechanics to the minutiae of sounds and utterances: what mattered, he stated, was not the letter but the spirit, not the detail but the overall picture, not one's memory but one's understanding.

The style of early Buddhist material is that of a 'religious' rather than a 'philosophical' tradition. Concerns that might be of philosophical interest to us at an intellectual level were overwhelmingly of existential and not abstract concern at that time. Indeed, the Buddha and his immediate followers, and other contemporary seekers of the truth, would all have been bemused by an attempt merely to intellectualize their ideas. The 5th-century BCE context nevertheless was the crucible in which the ideas and approaches of many different schools of thought were clearly formulated and established in relation to one another. Furthermore, it was from this century onwards that the assertions of the more influential approaches increasingly needed more systematic claims to validity. While the 5th-century BCE milieu might not itself have necessitated any formal explication of the theoretical underpinnings of the various different teachings, it was not long before formal explications were vying with one another for superiority and acceptance, and what had been taught either because of the injunctions of long-established tradition or for purely practical soteriological purposes acquired more scholastic and theoretical formulations and interpretations.

Chapter 4
Issues and Justifications
Language, grammar, and polemics

The Threat to the Brahmins

From the point of view of the brahmin priests, the developments that took place during the 5th century BCE posed a serious threat. The descendants of the Aryan invaders had been highly successful in establishing a dominant position both culturally and religiously, but the challenges of others during this period prompted the need for them to take serious steps to defend their practices and worldview. Most at risk was the sacrificial tradition. The competing views of others not only suggested that the rituals associated with the sacrifice were pointless, but would, if widely accepted, render the brahmins themselves redundant, and thus topple them from their place at the head of the hierarchy. What emerged in the brahmins' attempt to protect all aspects of their position was a reinforcement and formalization of a variety of technical arguments intended to demonstrate the validity and status of the sacrifice.

As with the developments of the 5th century BCE described in previous chapters, the formalizing of the Vedic 'defences' built on earlier trends. The ritual tradition was organized, preserved, and operated on the basis of specializations: different lineages were responsible for, and expert in, different specialist areas of the sacrifice as a whole. Thus the need to establish detailed arguments in defence of the ritual could draw on extant, as well as develop new, expertise: the act of defence was

Chronology

c.2000 BCE– : the Vedic sacrificial tradition.

c.800–500 BCE: the early Upaniṣads.

by 500 BCE: ritual and gnostic branches of the Brahmanical tradition coexisted.

5th-century BCE *milieu*: householders and renouncers.

c.485–405 BCE: the lifetime of the Buddha.

4th–2nd century BCE: In the face of proliferating counter-claims to knowledge of the truth, if the brahmins were to retain their hold on their dominant position they needed to clarify the issues which both justified their practices and confirmed their authority. As the ancient guardians of the sacrificial ritual and the language of Sanskrit, they sought to establish the criteria by which their practices and concerns would be validated, not just for themselves but also to refute the claims of others. In so doing they set the agenda for what each school of thought needed to establish in support of its own position.

Key figures include:

4th century BCE: the grammarian Pāṇini.

3rd–2nd century BCE: Kātyāyana and Patañjali, commentators on Pāṇini's grammar.

2nd century BCE: Jaimini, author of the first known exegetical text on the ritual section – karma-kāṇḍa – of the Veda.

2nd century BCE: Bādarāyāṇa, author of the *Brahma Sūtra*, an important exegetical text on the Upaniṣads – the jñāna-kāṇḍa of the Veda.

intricately interleaved with ongoing studies and supporting arguments within the Brahmanical tradition as a whole.

The Lines of Defence

Put simply, the threat to the ritual was primarily seen as a threat to the Veda itself – specifically the 'original', pre-Upaniṣadic action section (karma-kāṇḍa). Two lines of defence were thus necessary. The first was to reinforce and protect the continuity of the social hierarchy based on the ritual purity of its participants, on which depended the future of the Veda. Evidence of this social reinforcement is contained in treatises known as *Dharma-Śāstras* and *Artha-Śāstras*, which minutely detail and enjoin on each member of society their place, roles, duties, rights, aims, potential, and so on. Thus was fixed the social structure, and while extreme rigidity and exclusivity might be criticisms levelled against it, it nevertheless attained quite astonishing success in terms of longevity, persisting as it does to the present day. (It is perhaps worth noting that one reason for this is that in any given lifetime a person's position in the social hierarchy is believed to be determined by his or her actions (karma) in previous lives. This means that to insiders the system is based on the operating of a natural law rather than the accidentally elitist structure that Western eyes perceive it to be.)

The second was to preserve and defend the full extent of the material relating to the performance of ritual. Thus the specialisms that developed in this respect were based on disciplines known as the *vedāṅgas* – 'limbs of the Veda' – of which there were six. *Phonetics* was concerned with the correct pronunciation of the sounds uttered, chanted, or spoken at the sacrifice. *Metrics* was the classification of the metres of the various hymns or formulas of the sacrifice. *Grammar* was the establishing of the relations between component parts of sentences. *Etymological analysis* sought to explain the meaning of individual words within sentences. *Astronomy* established the most auspicious day and time for the performing of rituals. *Ceremonial rules* laid down the proper way for the various rituals of the sacrifice to be performed.

Astronomy and ceremonial rules apart, what the vedāṅgas also lent themselves to, that is of more interest to us, was the relating of the content of the Veda to an understanding of reality by means of *language*. That is to say, in establishing the rules of the language of the Veda, the way that language was operational in the world maintained by the sacrificial ritual was also established. This further meant that the nature of the world was explained, and that the relationship between language and knowledge of that world could be articulated – if only from this particular point of view. What follows will, I hope, show how these points emerge from the language debate.

Language and Reality

As became commonplace in many strands and aspects of the Indian traditions, over the centuries different theories and arguments were put forward within the Vedic tradition in support of the most important points in the debate on language: we need mention only some of the more significant of these here. Perhaps the most influential single figure was the great Indian grammarian Pāṇini, who lived during the 4th century BCE. Pāṇini wrote one of the most comprehensive and sophisticated grammars in the history of linguistics, highly respected to this day. His seminal work, the *Aṣṭādhyāyī*, comprises eight chapters containing 4000 rules. Together with appendices, the work covers all aspects of semantics, syntax, derivations, phonological rules, the classification of nominal and verbal roots, and rules for special cases. Pāṇini thus incorporated etymology and phonetics, also vedāṅgas in their own right and studied and written about separately by others, within his comprehensive grammar.

The language described by Pāṇini's grammar was Sanskrit, the language of the Veda and the language of the ritual. Sanskrit was considered 'ritually pure' speech, and of central importance was its creative aspect: the sound of the Sanskrit uttered at the sacrifice was believed to be what brought about the intended consequences of the sacrifice. Pāṇini's grammar explained this process as one of agency plus activity. Thus, for example, the creative import of a sentence such as 'water wets grain' is indicated by understanding it as 'wet grain is brought about by water'. For us, two things are noteworthy here. First is the point that the nominals (the naming words), in this case grain and water, are understood as substantives – actual things or beings. Second is that the agent, in this case water, need not be a conscious or intending actor: the sounds of the sacrifice are creatively effective as it were automatically, and certainly impersonally – the role of the priests in 'sounding the Vedic verses' being analogous to the water's in wetting the grain. Thus the language itself indicated the reality of the plural world in which the sacrifice was performed. And the essential part played by the priests preserving and guarding the texts of the ritual was confirmed: it was the language that was the creative instrument.

Of slightly tangential interest is the point that in codifying the grammatical rules of Sanskrit as he did, Pāṇini was instrumental in 'closing' the language. This is an unusual factor in the history of any language, as most continue to change and adapt in the context of cultural developments. Sanskrit, by contrast, has a specific 'classical' form, which provides a clear guide as to what is correct or incorrect, how it should or can be used, and so on. While it has had a rich tradition of use in the literature and drama of India as well as in other 'religious' writings, the point and justification of the rule-bound nature of Sanskrit is its unique status in the creative process of the sacrifice.

Two important followers of and commentators on Pāṇini were Patañjali and Kātyāyana, both of whom lived during the 2nd century BCE, whose contribution was to relate the Pāṇinian theoretical rules specifically to the way Sanskrit was used in practice. Usage constituted an additional grammatical authority, they stated. Indeed, usage constituted an authoritative means of knowledge. This was an important point because it meant that even apparently incomplete or imperfectly formed sentences could be understood by means of syntactic links. That is to say, if a sentence or series of words does not conform precisely to the minutiae of grammatical rules, it can be considered to be meaningful by means of usage conventions. It was an important assertion not only in extending the criteria by which language operated, but also more particularly for the defenders of the Veda. This was because not all of the material in the ritual texts was of a clear or consistent nature. A large part of it was comprised of injunctions (or, indeed, prohibitions), which were clearly indicated for the purposes of the ritual, and here the applicability of grammatical rules was obvious. But also contained in the texts were various supplementary descriptions whose meaning either was not self-evident or might be thought to be in conflict with statements made elsewhere in the texts. By means of usage criteria such passages could be interpreted as metaphors, or in other non-literal ways, ensuring the overall validity and coherence of the sacred language in which the texts were recorded.

Jaimini's Defence of the Veda

Eventually, theorizing on language and its role led other defenders of the Veda to much more specific attempts to establish the meaning and validity of the Veda's content. The work of the grammarians initially enabled them to ensure accurate preservation of the material and precision at the sacrifice itself. But it was also necessary to be able to argue that the entire corpus of material was meaningful and coherent. The first known important exegete of the Vedic texts, who attempted to understand the nature and purpose of the sacrificial ritual, was Jaimini, who lived during the 2nd century BCE. This was the beginning of the Mīmāṃsā tradition (*mīmāṃsā* means 'exegesis'). The proper name Mīmāṃsā came to be associated with exegesis of the ritual texts, the

Meaning and grammar

'Fire cooks rice.' This is a clear sentence, with two nominal substantives – fire and rice, an activity – cooking, and an agent – the fire which brings about the cooked rice. One can understand this as the 'creating' of cooked rice by means of the interaction between substantive entities and activity.

The meaning of individual words is linked to the overall grammatical form of the sentence. For example, if the above sentence was 'Fires cook rye', the different meaning of 'fires' (more than one fire) and 'rye' (a different substance is indicated by the different word) means that the sentence as a whole states something different from 'Fire cooks rice'. It is thus important to know both what each word means, which is the function of etymology, and how the grammatical rules work, if one is to understand the whole sentence.

'Her hair was pure sunlight.' This sentence cannot be taken literally, as it is not possible that hair can actually be sunlight. If the sentence was analysed according to etymological/grammatical rules (meaning of words linked with grammatical form), it would have to be rejected as erroneous. It can, however, be understood, by means of 'usage' rules, as a metaphor. It would thus be known that the point was that the hair in question was bright, shining, yellow-coloured, probably glowing or sparkling with light – and that no claim to its being actual sunlight was being made.

karma-kāṇḍha of the Veda, and the philosophical tradition based on such exegesis.

Our main discussion on Mīmāṃsā will take place in Chapter 8 because the flowering of the tradition came at a later date. But an understanding of its beginnings is helpful for us at this stage because of its influence on other schools of thought in intervening centuries. Jaimini's concern, recorded in his *Mīmāṃsā Sūtra*, was to understand the Vedic ritual texts as the codifiers of dharma. Dharma, as mentioned in Chapter 1, is the cosmic order maintained by the correct performance of the sacrifice, in turn dependent on the maintaining of the requisite social hierarchy. As an exegete of the ritual/dharma manuals, Jaimini defined dharma as having the nature of an injunction. That is to say, he interpreted the Vedic texts primarily in terms of their injunctive meaning: they told one what to do, or indeed not to do, at the sacrifice. The key point here was that he saw the texts in terms of their being solely the instigators of action(s). Everything contained in them, therefore, should be understood either literally as instructions to act, or as representing something related to this purpose. He accordingly used grammatical criteria to explain the way sentences should be understood to have injunctive meaning. He questioned the meaningfulness, and certainly

Dharma

Dharma is of central importance in the Brahmanical tradition. It is hard to translate into English without being misleading, so it is best to try to understand it conceptually. This has to be done on two 'levels'. Macrocosmically, it refers to cosmic order as a whole. Whatever there is is part of dharma in this sense. If things are not as they should be, or not arranged as optimally as they can be, a state of disorder or *a-dharma* exists: a breakdown in dharma.

Dharma is maintained in two ways: by means of the performing of sacrifices according to Vedic injunctions, and by means of individuals living according to their ritual social status and doing what they should do to maintain the optimum level of status quo in the social hierarchy. These constitute the second 'level', where one can see the microcosmic aspect of dharma, which refers to the duties of the individual. Individual dharma is called *sva-dharma*, one's 'own-dharma'. The correct performance of one's own-dharma is thus crucial if macrocosmic dharma is to be maintained and a-dharma prevented.

The rules of own-dharma were codified in great detail from the 2nd century BCE in texts known as the *Dharma-Śāstras*: the treatises on dharma-duty.

At a more philosophical level, the 2nd century BCE also saw the Vedic exegete Jaimini working on the primary dharma manuals – the much older Vedic ritual manuals. He stated that all of the Vedic texts consisted of injunctions to act, and he defined dharma in these terms: dharma is 'what should be done'.

From a more exclusively 'religious' perspective in the Hindu tradition, it is a breakdown in dharma (i.e. a-dharma) that necessitates and prompts divine intervention. In the text known as the *Bhagavad Gītā*, for example, an incarnated form of the supreme Godhead states: 'Whenever there is a breakdown in dharma I will come into being, in age after age.'

(*Bhagavad Gītā* IV, 7–8 – paraphrase)

the authority with regard to Vedic purpose, of anything that could not be explained in this way.

Jaimini took it that the injunctions related directly to actual substantives in the plural world. Drawing on the work of grammarians, he understood the meaning of a word to be correlated with the existence of the thing to which it refers. If one says 'cow', for example, in order for it to have meaning there must exist such a thing as a cow. Thus by definition the injunctions contained in the Veda meant that there must exist the necessary ingredients to bring them about: in each case at the very least the agent and the product. This meant that the Vedic texts reliably established both the reality of the cosmos to which they referred and the validity of the injunctions which must be performed in order to maintain the continuity of that cosmos.

Of the Upaniṣadic teaching that liberation is effected by knowledge of the essential identity of self and universe, Jaimini stated that it should be taken as an injunction to know one's self as performer of the sacrifice in relation to the universe one's actions were maintaining. He interpreted apparently monistic passages as metaphors, thus denying their incompatibility with the realism of the ritual material. Rather, he stated, the Upaniṣads established the reality of a plurality of individual selves, each of which needs to know that it exists as an agent.

The Primacy of the Upaniṣads

Alongside Jaimini's exegetical endeavours focused primarily on the ritual manuals, the Upaniṣads themselves were also specifically subjected to interpretation by those more interested in the non-ritual, 'know thyself' teachings expressed in them, but who were also concerned to establish the Vedic material as authoritative and superior to any other. An early version of an extremely important text (later adapted by others), purporting to summarize the key teachings of the Upaniṣads as they should be understood, was written by Bādarāyaṇa, a contemporary of Jaimini. Bādarāyaṇa's text is commonly known as the *Vedānta Sūtra*, reflecting the fact that the Upaniṣads form the 'end of the Veda' (*vedānta*). The text is also known as the *Brahma Sūtra*, indicating that its major concern is not ritual but understanding what the Upaniṣads have to say about Brahman, the ground of the cosmos. The first verse of the text proclaims: 'Then [there is] the enquiry into Brahman', and the second verse continues: 'that from which [occurs] the origin, maintenance, and dissolution [of all that there is]'. This suggests not just a different focus, but also a profoundly different understanding of the nature of reality. In place of the plurality insisted upon in Jaimini's work, the *Vedānta Sūtra* indicates that all things are part of the one Brahman. This implies that ritual injunctions should not be taken, as suggested by Jaimini, to indicate the reality of what they refer to: for Bādarāyaṇa, language does not have this substantively indicative nature. Furthermore, as injunctive texts in their own right, the Upaniṣads state that what one should 'do' is know Brahman.

Text and Testimony

Jaimini's and Bādarāyaṇa's works became the seminal texts of the later Mīmāṃsā and Vedānta darśanas respectively. For this reason Mīmāṃsā and Vedānta are sometimes referred to as Purva (early) and Uttara (late) Mīmāṃsā (exegesis) – that is, exegesis of the early and late sections of the Veda respectively. Between them they also established two important features of the Indian tradition as a whole. First was their style of writing, the extremely cryptic 'sūtra' form. Each verse consists of just a few words whose meaning and context are often far from self-evident, and the texts require further interpretation if they are to be understood. It is possible that this reflects the fact that the tradition was primarily an oral one, the key points argued by important figures merely being recorded in the form of an aide-mémoire. It might also reflect a tendency to exclusivity of understanding in each tradition, indicating the superiority of those 'in-the-know'. Whatever it was that prompted its use, an important consequence of the cryptic style was that over time more than one school of thought emerged within each tradition as later exegetes added their own commentaries to the early texts.

The second feature that was established by these two early exegetes

The cryptic nature of the Sūtras

It must in fact be eternal, as it is spoken for another's sake. There is always correspondence. Because there is no number. Because it is independent.

(*Mīmāṃsā Sūtra* 1.1.18–21 – on the nature of language)

Then there is the enquiry into Brahman. From which is the origin, etc., of this. This from its being the origin of the texts. And that because it is associated with their purpose.

(*Vedānta Sūtra* 1.1.1–4 – on the subject matter of the Sūtra)

was the beginnings of what was to become an extremely important, and controversial, epistemological criterion in the Indian tradition – testimony. That is to say, rejecting absolutely the teachings of the Buddha and others, both Jaimini and Bādarāyaṇa stated that the Vedic sources represented an unquestionably valid source of knowledge: what they said was to be taken as wholly reliable. Epistemological criteria came to be known by the Sanskrit term *pramāṇa*, 'means of knowing', and testimony was called *śabda-pramāṇa*, literally 'knowing by means of word'. From this time on, the extent to which testimony could be accepted as a valid means of knowledge had to be considered by each systematic thinker, whether the source in question was the Veda, something else, or someone else's 'word'. Those who either rejected the reliability of testimony, or gave it low epistemological priority, had to establish the primacy and validity of at least one other epistemological criterion, such as perception, inference, or reasoning/logical argument. Related ontological issues also had to be considered and argued for: in particular, the nature and 'reality status' of self – in relation to knowing and agency, and the nature and 'reality status' of world – in relation to what is known and/or acted upon. In some cases, consideration was also given to whether or not these were related to, or could be determined by, the use of language.

The investigation of issues to do with the self came to be known by the term *ātma-vidyā* – the 'knowledge of the self'. And the activity of philosophizing in general was referred to by the term *ānvīkṣikī*, which means something like 'looking at', or even 'what to look at'. It is usually understood as a technical term for 'logical reasoning', but the term in fact reflects the early stages during which the tradition was literally deciding and establishing what should be 'looked at', 'kept in view', 'the subject of enquiry'. Any theory put forward needed to be, or at least to claim to be, internally coherent and consistent in these respects. Further, criticisms of others' views focused on their handling and understanding of these issues. Ānvīkṣikī was concerned with how this enterprise was conducted.

In the milieu of debate that ensued, it was common for the proponent of a theory to put forward first an alternative view, which he would then proceed to deny. The alternative view (sometimes more than one are included for denial in a single argument) was referred to as that of the *pūrva-pakṣin*, the 'earlier proponent'. Commonly, this was expressed as: 'If it is said [i.e. if the pūrva-pakṣin says] that X (or Y, or Z), then this is wrong.' Though precise details varied from system to system, the denial and argument would then proceed, focusing not just on the alternative views as such but also on the epistemological criteria by which they have been arrived at. The current proponent would also put forward his own position with whatever supporting evidence was appropriate to his approach and view, and explain his own epistemological criteria.

Chapter 5

Categories and Method

Vaiśeṣika and Nyāya

Vaiśeṣika Thought: the Categories of the Cosmos

One of the first systems of thought to emerge from the early milieu of deciding 'what to look at' was that of Kaṇāda, as recorded in his *Vaiśeṣika Sūtra*, written during the 2nd century BCE. Though his origins and background are of uncertain orthodoxy, Kaṇāda, like Jaimini, was concerned with understanding dharma. For Kaṇāda, dharma was supreme, to the extent that unlike Jaimini, who believed the Veda itself to be self-validatingly supreme, Kaṇāda upheld the Veda (only) because it upheld dharma. That is to say, while Jaimini was primarily a Vedic exegete and defender of the Veda, Kaṇāda was most interested in the nature of reality, which he understood as dharma, and which happened to be maintained by the putting into practice of the Vedic injunctions. Thus the opening verses of the *Vaiśeṣika Sūtra* state:

> We shall now consider the nature of dharma.
> It is from dharma that the highest and supreme good is achieved.
> The Veda has its authority because of its concern with dharma.
>
> (*Vaiśeṣika Sūtra* 1–3)

The *Vaiśeṣika Sūtra* represents a system of pluralistic realism: the independent reality of each of the objects of the world about us, outside of and separate from ourselves. What it is concerned with is the

Chronology

c.2000 BCE– : the Vedic sacrificial tradition.

c.800–500 BCE: the early Upaniṣads.

by 500 BCE: ritual and gnostic branches of the Brahmanical tradition coexisted.

5th-century BCE *milieu*: householders and renouncers.

c.485–405 BCE: the lifetime of the Buddha.

4th – 2nd century BCE: grammarians and early exegetes establish what should be 'looked at'.

3rd – 2nd century BCE: Kaṇāda's *Vaiśeṣika Sūtra* – concerned with the ontological status of the 'particulars' (*viśeṣa*) of reality. Kaṇāda sought to establish of what 'particulars', or types of entity, the world is comprised.

c.3rd century CE: Gotama's *Nyāya Sūtra* – adopting Kaṇāda's ontology of pluralistic realism, Nyāya was concerned with how one can arrive at certain knowledge of that realism – what are the valid means of knowledge? Its main contribution was an epistemological method, based on inferential reasoning.

investigation of that plurality in order to classify it according to the different types of entity of which it is comprised. This is where the system gets its name, as 'Vaiśeṣika' indicates the particularities (*viśeṣa*) under investigation. The lasting influence of Vaiśeṣika's approach and ontology is felt by virtue of its close association with the Nyāya system of thought, first propounded by a man named Gotama, whose dates are uncertain but who probably lived around the 3rd century CE. Combined together into what tends to be known as Nyāya-Vaiśeṣika, they have played an extremely important and influential role among the classical darśanas, making major contributions to Indian thought. Even though the more dominant Nyāya is often referred to or studied on its own, such an approach presupposes its adoption of Vaiśeṣika realism. So it is helpful to have some understanding of the Vaiśeṣika position and claims before looking at Nyāya, as well as a feeling of the detailed extent to which their claim to realism was analytically presented.

The classification of particularities with which Vaiśeṣika was concerned was undertaken in terms of ascertaining the fundamental 'categories' of all existent entities. The Sanskrit term for such categories was *padārtha*, which literally means 'what is predicated by the word', in itself taken as indicating the transcendental reality of the entities under investigation. That is, by virtue of being verbally referred to, an object is understood to have independent existence. According to Vaiśeṣika there are seven categories: substance, quality, action, universality, particularity, a relation of inherence, and (added later) absence or negation.

Substance and Quality

The most important of these categories is substance, because all the other categories in some way relate to it. All substance of whatever nature is reducible to one or other of nine different kinds: earth, water, fire, air, ether, space, time, self, and mind. Each is characterized by different qualities, and of the first five the *Vaiśeṣika Sūtra* states:

> Earth possesses colour, taste, smell, and touch [as well as solidity],
> Water possesses colour, taste, touch, and fluidity,
> Fire possesses colour and touch [as well as heat],
> Air possesses touch [as well as mobility].
> Ether possesses no perceivable qualities.
>
> (*Vaiśeṣika Sūtra* II.1.1–5 – paraphrase)

Vaiśeṣika ontology is one of pluralistic realism. It breaks down the fundamental constituents of reality into 7 **categories**: substance, quality, action, universality, particularity, a relation of inherence, and absence or negation.

Substance is further subdivided into 9 different kinds of 'atoms': earth, water, fire, air, ether, space, time, self, and mind.

Earth, water, fire, and air are **material substance** atoms; ether, space, time, self, and mind are **immaterial substance** atoms. All atoms are eternal.

Earth, water, fire, and air atoms group together to form recognizable objects, in association, where appropriate, with one or more of the other atoms. Ether, space, time, and self are, as well as being eternal, all-pervading. Mind, however, is only atomic in size, and one mind atom is associated with a single self atom in each individual human being.

Substance is the most important category as it is only in relation to substance that the other categories occur.

There are 24 **qualities**, and 5 kinds of **action**, that **inhere** in **substances.** Each individual occurrence of a **substance** is a **particular** example of a **universality. Absence** allows for various kinds of negation, non-presence, or non-existence to be understood as part of reality.

Though unperceivable, the principal quality of ether is that it is the medium through which sounds, for example, travel and reach the senses. As such it is a substance in its own right.

All substances occur in atomic form, each atom being eternal and indestructible. It is in joining together in varying proportions that these atoms produce all the various objects of the universe, which are in turn finite and reducible to their constituent atoms. Unlike earth, water, fire, and air, which constitute material substance, the atoms of ether, space, time, self, and mind are immaterial. Of these five immaterial substances, mind is particular to each individual self and is itself of atomic size, whereas the remaining four, as well as being eternal, are omnipresent substances.

The plurality of selves is indicated by the plural manifestation of the quality of consciousness (or cognition), and each self is further characterized by the qualities desire, aversion, pleasure, pain, and effort. The part mind plays, and its existence is inferred from its activity, is in processing sensory information: it is also instrumental in allowing the self to be internally perceived. This distinct separation of self and mind is not uncommon in Indian thought.

In outlining the category of substance, we have already referred to examples of the second category listed, quality. Qualities can only reside in substances and cannot occur on their own. Between 17 and 24 qualities are listed in different Vaiśeṣika texts, and they are subdivided into those qualities that can reside in material substances, those that can reside in immaterial substances, and those that can reside in both. Thus those such as colour, taste, smell, touch, fluidity, and solidity, for example, reside in the material substances earth, water, fire, and air; those such as cognition, happiness, unhappiness, desire, and aversion reside only in the immaterial substances; number, magnitude, and conjunction, for example, reside in any substance. Sometimes more than one substance needs to be present for a particular quality to inhere, such as conjunction, otherness, and plural number.

The importance of qualities is that they characterize substance in such a way as to render substance identifiable to us as this or that object. Without qualities, substance would not be distinguishable in terms of the world as we know it. Thus substance always has at least one quality inhering in it. And this inherence is itself a further category in the Vaiśeṣika schema, acting as what one might call a kind of 'glue' between two other categories, which otherwise could not exist on their own. An example often given to illustrate this point is the impossibility of the quality 'colour' occurring on its own, or the composite substance 'rose' occurring without the quality colour. Thus if we take in this case a red rose, the colour red necessarily inheres as a quality in the substance rose. In spite of the necessity of the relationship, however, quality (in this case colour) and substance (in this case rose), as well as inherence, are categorially separate aspects of reality.The colour red can also be used to illustrate the categories of universality and particularity. The red inhering in an individual red rose is a particular example of the universal 'redness'. A universal may be common to any number of particulars, and it is the particularity of the individual occurrence of the universal that differentiates one rose, say, from another. Moreover, it is only by means of particularity that universality can manifest. Even individual ontologically identical atoms, ranging from all earth atoms to all self atoms, are differentiated by particularity in this radically pluralistic schema: in spite of being categorially alike, and sharing in common universality, each is in some sense unique, and this is separately categorized as its particularity. The importance of universality is that without it, there would be no way of knowing that certain particulars – say, all roses – share in a common rose-ness: that, while each is particular, they all are in fact roses.

Of the remaining two categories we need to discuss, action and absence, action is the more important, since it represents the active and dynamic aspect of substance where qualities are passive and inactive. Action accounts for all obvious activity, as well as the way in which atoms become, and cease to be, composite objects. In this latter respect, action is required in addition to inherence, acting as the 'causative' factor. It is action that accounts for causation as a whole, and one could almost conceptually substitute 'causation' for 'action' as the name of this category – though the Vaiśeṣikas themselves never did so.

The counting of absence as a separate category might be considered surprising in such a wholeheartedly realistic school of thought. It was added to the original list of six categories in order to include the indication of absence or non-existence as a true and 'real' state of affairs in a system in which existence was thought to be an intrinsic attribute of the object under investigation – reality. Thus the category 'absence' allowed for statements such as 'there is no rose here' and 'ether possesses no perceivable qualities' to have real meaning. Five kinds of absence were identified: there is no rose here (absence); a rose is not a cow (difference); there is no flower yet on the rosebush (non-existence prior to existence); the rose is no more (non-existence following existence); roseness is never found in a cow (something that never exists). It was because absence is as it were a part of reality in this way that it was accorded its own separate category.

It is not known exactly how the Vaiśeṣikas arrived at their ontology: that is, it is unclear whether they were attempting to describe reality, or whether they were attempting to construct a reality-structure system. So it is not known where they got the categorial system from, or what criteria they used in order to determine the inclusion in the system of its different factors. When the Naiyāyikas adopted Vaiśeṣika's ontological system they do not seem to have questioned this either. What one can say of both schools, however, is that they sought to establish the ultimate reality of the plural world of common sense, and that they accepted common-sense perceptions as providing a true representation of that world, however they then chose to categorize it. They thus gave high priority to sense perception as a means of knowing, in contrast with Jaimini's and Bādarāyaṇa's dependence on testimony. This acceptance of the validity of the everyday world of sense perception did, however, endorse the ontological stance of the Vedic exegetes, but it was subsequently questioned by others – notably by Buddhists, as we shall see in the next chapter.

The Contribution of Nyāya

The Nyāya thinkers, beginning with Gotama in his *Nyāya Sūtra*, added to the Vaiśeṣika system two highly significant factors. The first is that they established clear criteria according to which it could be logically demonstrated that each factor of the system is as it is described as being. That is, they introduced a particular 'method', based on specific rules of reasoning, by which certain knowledge could be arrived at with regard to the object of enquiry. This allowed them to claim that they had 'proved' the pluralistic reality that perceptions present to us. It is worth mentioning that as well as sense perceptions, Nyāya accepted the validity of the yogic perception mentioned in Chapter 1, as well as other, what one might loosely call 'intuitive', kinds of perception. But of all of these, it is sense perceptions that play the most important epistemological role for Naiyāyikas. Nyāya's formal method was the earliest to emerge in the flourishing milieu of debate in ancient India, and the rules it established had a lasting influence on the tradition as a whole. It also contributed to the rules of debate more generally, in the sense of stating what makes an argument invalid or disallowable.

The second significant factor the Nyāya thinkers added to the Vaiśeṣika system was that they stated that the knowledge gained in this way was soteriologically efficacious (that is, its acquisition affected the destiny of believers) – something the Vaiśeṣikas had not explicitly concerned themselves with, possibly because Kaṇāda was more interested in dharma (as the structure of the cosmos) than in mokṣa (liberation). In introducing his method for arriving at certain knowledge, Gotama states that it should only be used in certain circumstances. He gives a list of 'objects of true knowledge', which consists of those things the existence and nature of which it is legitimate to enquire into – because knowledge concerning them contributes to attainment of the 'highest good', understood in this tradition to mean liberation.

> Certain knowledge concerning the proper means of valid knowledge and those objects it is legitimate to enquire into . . . [and other relevant factors with regard to method and procedure in debate] leads to the attainment of the highest good.
>
> It is the removal of false knowledge that . . . [eventually, after several stages] leads to liberation.
>
> (*Nyāya Sūtra* 1.1.1–2)

We will discuss the Nyāya method with reference, first, to the criteria it laid down for the undertaking of an enquiry, and, second, to its list of the valid objects of enquiry. This will lead us into a discussion of the way it deals with specific examples from that list.

How to Proceed

Enquiry should be undertaken, Nyāya states, only if some doubt exists as to what is to be enquired into. That is, there is no point in conducting an enquiry if something is already known for certain. What is enquired into must, therefore, be something about which there might be different understandings. Furthermore, there must be some possibility of a certain outcome to the enquiry. The aim of the enquiry is certain knowledge, which constitutes a 'conclusion' of the enquiry, and if it would be impossible to arrive at this then conducting the enquiry is itself pointless. It is the possibility of arriving at hitherto unknown certainty that both indicates the required previous state of uncertainty, or doubt, and is one of the key validating points of undertaking the enquiry.

Doubt and the possibility of certainty are not, however, on their own enough to legitimate undertaking an enquiry. If they were, then one might be motivated by mere curiosity, and such 'aimlessness', Gotama states, is contrary to man's 'rational behaviour'. Rather, there must also be a proper 'purpose' to the undertaking. Though open to different interpretations at various stages of the tradition, the implication of this statement in the Nyāya Sūtra, that the enquiry must contribute to the attaining of the 'highest good', is that the purpose should be to contribute to gaining liberation from rebirth.

Another requirement for the undertaking of an enquiry is that there must be some observational data that can be used in support both of the proposition made at the outset of the enquiry and of the supporting criteria of the argument establishing certainty. It is here that the Nyāya system most specifically relates itself to drawing on what it takes to be the reality of the plural world about us. The point, for Naiyāyikas, is that in making use of observational data, such as 'where there is smoke, there is fire', they claim to be establishing support that is beyond dispute, thus cementing the validity and finality of the conclusion of the argument. This feature of the system also shows the importance for Nyāya of linking observational data, or the empirical world, into their system of logical argument. There is no place for philosophical abstractions based only on, say, mathematical logic, as found in modern Western philosophy. Rather, their logical method is grounded in the world around them, and the human beings in it, in a much more existential or experiential sense.

The Method Itself

This brings us to the method itself, which is given as an argument with five stages or 'limbs', which lead the enquiry to a certain conclusion. The five stages are: first, a statement of the thesis which is to be proven; second, the statement of a reason for the thesis; third, the giving of an example which acts as a 'rule' which can be drawn on in support of proving the thesis; fourth, the relating of the 'rule' to the thesis; and fifth, a restatement of the thesis as thus proven. The example given by Gotama in the *Nyāya Sūtra* is: (1) There is fire on the hill; (2) Because there is smoke there; (3) Where there is smoke there is fire (as one can see in the kitchen); (4) There is smoke, which is associated with fire, on the hill; (5) Therefore there is fire on the hill.

From this five-limbed method can be seen the crucial importance attributed by Nyāya to inference: it can be inferred that there is X (fire on the hill), such inference being based on observational evidence Y (smoke) and rule Z (where there is smoke there is fire). Inferential reasoning and the use of data acquired by means of perception constitute the primary means of arriving at certain knowledge for Nyāya. Later in the Indian tradition as a whole, notably by Buddhist logicians as well as later Naiyāyikas, more attention was paid to ascertaining the reliability of the examples or 'rules' on which inference was based, such as whether smoke is in fact a reliable indication of fire. This development was important because the rule was meant to be invariable, such that it constituted absolutely reliable support for the proving of the thesis proposition. But notwithstanding the loophole in his system, it was the author of the early *Nyāya Sūtra*, Gotama, who, as well as contributing the first formal philosophical method, first laid down the central place of inference in a logical argument in this way.

We can now turn to the valid objects of enquiry as listed by Gotama. The list is in addition to the Vaiśeṣika categories of substance and so on, and is given in *Nyāya Sūtra* 1.1.9 as: self, body, sense organs, sense objects, cognition, mind, action, defects, cyclical birth and death, consequences, suffering, and liberation. Vātsyāyana, an important successor of Gotama, clearly wishing to establish the coherence of the list, comments on it as follows:

> Here, the self is the seer of all things, enjoyer of all things, omniscient, experiencer of all things. Body is the place of the self's pleasure and pain.

> The sense organs are the means by which pleasure and pain are cognized. The internal sense 'mind' is that which knows all objects. Action is the cause of all pleasure and pain; so are the defects of desire, envy, and attachment. The self had earlier bodies, and will have other bodies after this one, until liberation is achieved. It is this that is the beginningless cycle of birth and death. 'Consequence' is the experiencing of pleasure and pain, along with their means, pain being inextricably linked with pleasure. In order to achieve liberation, one has to understand all happiness as the same as pain; this gives rise to detachment and, eventually, liberation.
>
> (*Nyāya Sūtra Bhāṣya*: Commentary on *Nyāya Sūtra* 1.1.9)

In the context of the criteria given by Gotama for undertaking any enquiry, this list informs us of those things he thought it was justifiable to want to arrive at certain knowledge of, and about which there is, prior to any enquiry, an element of doubt as to their existence and/or nature. Knowledge about these things would, further, contribute to the 'highest good', which is the main purpose of the enterprise.

Proof of the Self

As an example of the way Gotama applies the method he lays down in his *Nyāya Sūtra* to the items on his list of valid objects of enquiry, let us look at his 'proof' of the existence of the essential self (ātman). This object of enquiry clearly fulfils the criterion of doubt, since there was far from being a consensus as to its existence and nature. On the contrary, it featured high on the agenda of those engaged in the religio-philosophical quest. The Naiyāyikas believed that the application of their method would produce conclusive certain knowledge of the existence of an essential self, and that acquiring this knowledge would be beneficial in the quest for the highest good. In looking at this example, one can also see the way the Naiyāyikas drew on the Vaiśeṣika system of substance and qualities.

Gotama puts forward the thesis that there is a plurality of selves. The reason he gives is that there is a plurality of consciousnesses, and there also exist plurally the qualities of desire, hatred, effort, pleasure, and pain. The example or rule cited is that a plurality of consciousnesses, together with these particular qualities, indicates immaterial, eternal selves that are separate from both the mind and the body: precisely these, in other words, are the characteristics of this kind of self. All of these characteristics are the case, indicating a plurality of selves. Therefore there is a plurality of selves. The sūtra in which the existence of the self is proclaimed (*Nyāya Sūtra* 1.1.10) is very cryptic, and its commentary, in which the argument is more fully stated, is not a model of clarity, so each methodological point requires a degree of drawing out. But this nevertheless is the shape of the 'proof' given for this object of enquiry. It is also stated that the qualities only inhere in the self prior to liberation from rebirth, after which each self is free from all qualities but retains its individuality, which is eternal. In a clear reference to the Vedic textual exegetical traditions, Nyāya claims that this is a far more certain way of knowing about the self than relying on testimony.

Needless to say, this and the other 'proofs' given in the *Nyāya Sūtra* and its commentaries, such as those for the separate plurality and nature of 'minds', were subjected to all manner of critiques by contemporary and later thinkers. The method, however, has been taken seriously to this day, both within the Indian tradition and also in Western philosophical circles, where it has provided one of the most accessible aspects of the Indian tradition to extrapolate for consideration in the context of Western thought. Among other things, modern scholars have debated its structure and relative methodological merits in comparison with Aristotle's syllogism, frequently exemplified as: 'All men are mortal; Socrates is a man; therefore Socrates is mortal.'

To sum up, the Nyāya-Vaiśeṣika view of the world is one of pluralistic realism. They take it that the perceiving of something conveys to the perceiver knowledge of the independent existence of that thing: if one sees, say, a rose, then one can take it that the rose is transcendentally real. This means that it is not just the qualities that inhere in the rose, such as redness and a sweet smell, that are knowable by means of sensory perception, but also the rose itself as a separately existing substance. This realism is reliable enough for it to function as the basis of the Nyāya system of inferential reasoning in order to acquire certain knowledge of the existence and nature of other, more important and soteriologically significant, things such as eternal selves and minds, that are not knowable by means of perception alone. Thus the main means of knowing utilized in the Nyāya-Vaiśeṣika darśana(s) are perception, reasoning, and inference.

Chapter 6
Things and No-things
Developments in Buddhist thought

We saw in Chapter 4 the way in which the advent of challenging alternative teachings and ideas prompted orthodox brahmins to attempt to defend the validity and authority of the Vedic material, both the ritual manuals and the Upaniṣads. And we have seen how this was to influence the pluralistic realism of the more systematic Nyāya-Vaiśeṣika discourses. Alongside these developments taking place under the umbrella of the Brahmanical tradition, Buddhist thought and teachings were also being subjected to scrutiny, adaptation, study, and revision. Before embarking on a discussion of these, it is worth mentioning that, both internally and in relation to other schools of thought, many of the ideas and arguments put forward by Buddhist thinkers can seem very difficult for the beginner to grasp. I hope, however, that the broader context this chapter will cover will help in clarifying any problems the reader may encounter. The profundity of Buddhist philosophy is also worthy of perseverance: it contains some of the most radical propositions in the history of human thought.

Varieties of Buddhist Thought

Within the Buddhist tradition the first serious debates concerned the monastic disciplinary rules, leading both to their acceptance and codification by some and to their rejection and revision by others. In this so-called 'schismatic' way began the early splintering of Buddhism into different 'schools': their initial disciplinary differences paved the way for differences in doctrinal outlook to emerge and take root among like-minded communities. Texts refer to some 18 schools which existed in India at various stages during the 800 years or so following the death of the Buddha. Of these, which might collectively be referred to as representing 'early' or 'pre-Mahāyāna' Buddhism, only Theravāda Buddhism survives to the present day, but others about which we have

Chronology

c.2000 BCE– : the Vedic sacrificial tradition.

c.800–500 BCE: the early Upaniṣads.

by 500 BCE: ritual and gnostic branches of the Brahmanical tradition coexisted.

5th-century BCE milieu: householders and renouncers.

c.485–405 BCE: the lifetime of the Buddha.

4th–2nd century BCE: grammarians and early exegetes establish the criteria of what should be 'looked at'.

3rd–2nd century BCE: Vaiśeṣika and Nyāya combine an ontology of pluralistic realism and a formal method by which to arrive at certain knowledge.

4th–1st century BCE: the early Buddhist tradition undergoes division into different schools. Initially based on different disciplinary codes, these gradually developed distinctively different doctrinal views.

3rd century BCE–2nd century CE: development of the Buddhist *Abhidharma* (in Pāli *Abhidhamma*) tradition: the scholastic activity of the investigation and categorizing of phenomena (dharmas/dhammas) in order to understand the nature of reality.

1st century BCE–*1st century* CE: the emergence of Mahāyāna Buddhism and the early *Prajñāpāramitā* ('Perfection of Wisdom') *Sūtras*.

c.*2nd century* CE: drawing on *Prajñāpāramitā* literature, Nāgārjuna's *Madhyamaka Kārikā* focus on the 'emptiness' (*śūnyatā*) of all phenomena, and establish the basis of the Madhyamaka (Middle Way) school of thought. Of central importance to Nāgārjuna's teachings is the Buddha's doctrine of 'dependent origination'.

c.*4th century* CE: the Cittamātra ('Mind Only'), or Yogācāra ('Practice of Yoga'), school of Buddhism establishes an alternative interpretation of the import of the *Prajñāpāramitā* teachings, seeking to redress the apparent nihilism of the 'emptiness' school. As suggested by the terms 'yoga' and 'mind', its approach centres on understanding meditative processes, or 'consciousness events'.

information include the Lokottaravādins, the Sammatīyas, the Sautrāntikas, and the Sarvāstivādins.

The criteria on which schools were doctrinally divided related to the ontological status of persons (in this case either the Buddha specifically or all human beings) and the world, themes common to the wider Indian milieu. The brahmins and the Nyāya-Vaiśeṣikas in some respects had a simpler starting point because their position accorded with a common-sense view of reality. But the Buddhists had to contend with initial teachings that focused on mental processes rather than the external world, and, what is more problematic, the teaching of 'not-self'.

For Lokottaravādins, the main issue was the status of the historical Buddha. Most Buddhists accepted that he was a man of the same status as any other, but the Lokottaravādins held that in some way he transcended normal humanity, and thus was not subject to the Buddhist metaphysical criterion of impermanence. (*Lokottara* is a compound of the words *loka*, 'world', and *uttara*, 'beyond' or 'above'.) Many later Buddhists came to believe in the transcendence of the Buddha, as well as that of other great figures of compassion and insight known as Bodhisattvas, but the Lokottaravādins were alone among early Buddhists in holding this view. Its significance for adherents was that the goal they hoped to achieve by following the teachings was a supramundane one.

Schools and texts of Buddhism

Textual sources suggest that during the 500 years following the lifetime of the Buddha, some 18 different schools of Buddhism were established. Initial 'schism' in the monastic group was based on disagreement over disciplinary rules, like-minded groups subsequently also interpreting teachings differently. The only early school of Buddhism to survive to the modern day is **Theravāda Buddhism.** Other early schools include the **Lokottaravādins**, the **Sammatīyas**, the **Sautrāntikas**, and the **Sarvāstivādins.**

Canonical texts are of three kinds:

- doctrinal treatises – **Suttas** or **Sūtras**
- monastic disciplinary codes – **Vinaya**
- scholastic interpretation of teachings – **Abhidharma**

Extant **Abhidharmas** relate to the **Theravāda** and **Sarvāstivāda** schools.

The **Sautrāntikas** specifically adhere only to **sūtra** texts and reject the scholastic approach of other schools.

The Sammatīyas claimed that, notwithstanding the 'not-self' doctrine (which most interpreted as 'there is no self'), all human beings did have some kind of personal selfhood. No evidence remains of how this was thought to be constituted, but the views of Sammatīyas were roundly rejected by other Buddhists.

Abhidharma

The name of the Sautrāntika school (*sūtra-āntika*) indicates that the corpus of teachings this group accepted as most authoritative was that contained in the doctrinal treatises or Sūtras. They saw this distinction to be necessary because of the development of more scholastic, interpretive treatises contained in works known as the Abhidharmas. Both the Theravāda and Sarvāstivāda schools had their own Abhidharma: that of the Theravādins is extant in Pāli (the *Abhidhamma Piṭaka*) and that of the Sarvāstivādins is in Sanskrit. (As the brahmins engaged with others in defending their material, Sanskrit became the lingua franca of debate and text-writing in India, but all extant Theravāda works, preserved in Ceylon (now Sri Lanka) rather than in mainland India, are in Pāli.)

The Abhidharma tradition was concerned with (*abhi*) *dharma*(*s*). This 'concern with dharma' is seen in two ways. First, it relates to the understanding and definitive interpretation of the teachings (Dharma) as a whole. This was thought necessary because of the cryptic or ambiguous nature of the way the teachings were first presented, leading some to feel that the tradition required some kind of codified clarification. Words, phrases, sentences, and doctrinal teachings were subjected to close analysis and 'correct' definitions and interpretations were recorded. Second, the Abhidharmikas investigated the nature of reality in terms of 'dharmas'. Whatever there is, of whatever nature, can be referred to neutrally and non-predicatively as a dharma. That is to say, the term dharma does not in itself confer on to its referents any quality or status whatsoever. In Chapter 3 we saw the term used in this way (in Pāli) in the third line of the Three Marks of Existence formula: 'all dhammas are not-self'. The Abhidharmikas sought, then, to establish the nature of reality in the context of the Buddha's teachings in much the same way that Gotama's *Vaiśeṣika Sūtra* sought to do in the context of Vedic Dharma (confusingly, yet another use of the word Dharma).

Dharma again

In Brahmanical thought, dharma means both cosmic order and one's personal duty, as explained in the box on page 64–5. In Buddhism, dharma (Pāli *dhamma*) also has two important meanings. In the first instance, it refers to the teachings of the Buddha. On becoming a Buddhist, a person agrees to 'take refuge in' (i.e. accept, respect, and be loyal to) the Buddha, his teachings (the Dharma), and the community. Second, and of more importance to us here, dharma is the term used to refer loosely and generically to 'everything', without indicating anything about it. It is an umbrella term, applicable equally to concrete and abstract, immediate or remembered, sensory or conceptual, subjective or objective, sentient or insentient, organic or inorganic, and so on. The term first appears in this way in the early Buddhist teaching that 'all dhammas are anattā (not self)', discussed in Chapter 3.

The Sautrāntikas did not reject the validity of the efforts of the Abhidharmikas, but they gave priority to analysing and understanding the nature of reality as suggested in the teachings contained in the earlier doctrinal treatises (known as Sūtras), rather than developing a scholastic tradition. Their analysis centred on explaining the relationship between one's cognitive experience of the world and karmic continuity. The constituents of this experiential process (dharmas) were, they stated, impermanent, changing, and 'momentary', without any kind of inherent existence. In taking this stance the Sautrāntikas engaged particularly with the Sarvāstivādins, whose worldview was based almost entirely on their Abhidharma, a comprehensive work that seeks to establish that 'everything exists', which is the meaning of *sarva asti*.

In proceeding in their investigations, the Abhidharmikas of both schools attributed the 'not-self' doctrine in effect exclusively to human beings rather than to all dharmas alike. They did this by stating that human beings were comprised not of an independent self but of five coexisting constituent parts called *skandhas* (in Pāli, *khandhas*) – the same fivefold structure that was explained in Chapter 3 as the cognitive apparatus. These constituents were themselves subject to dharma analysis, but constituted the doctrine by which Buddhists rejected any claim by others to any kind of independent or persisting human selfhood.

The Sarvāstivādins were also exercised particularly by the reality status of dharmas in relation to continuity. How could there be any kind of causative link between impermanent dharmas, how could one understand the mutual relationship between impermanence and continuity? They answered such questions by claiming that while all dharmas are momentary, existing long enough only to effect continuity, they are also actually existent in all 'time modes' – past, present, and future. They attributed to dharmas a continuing fundamental 'essence' (*svabhāva*, 'own-being'), going so far as to refer to them as 'substance'.

The Theravādin Abhidharmikas pursued their investigation of dharmas not in terms of time-modes but by categorizing all aspects of experience in terms of kinds of dharmas. In this way they sought to make sense of why there are phenomenologically significant distinctions between, say, concrete and abstract aspects of experience. In all, the Theravādins categorized dharmas into some 28 'physical' and 52 'mental' categories, plus consciousness. The point for practitioners was to learn to observe and analyse them in meditative states, thus facilitating the attainment of insight.

The decline of Buddhism in India

For about a millennium after the death of the Buddha, Buddhism flourished in India. During the reign of the Maurya king Aśoka, in the 3rd century BCE, Buddhism became the official state religion of India and its monastic communities were heavily endowed. This led to the establishment of a strong community base in which ideas could proliferate and from which the Buddhist teachings could be spread. For centuries, Buddhist thought played a major role in the religio-philosophical life of India, contributing a variety of original and sophisticated ideas, critiques, and points of view. Many of these were conveyed to other countries, such as Ceylon (now Sri Lanka), China, and Tibet (and via these to South East Asia and the Far East), establishing Buddhism as a major world religion. It is not known for certain how or why Buddhism virtually died out in India. There are a number of possibilities: that it became top-heavy, with insufficient lay members to sustain its continuity; that the proliferation of devotional cults within what we now call Hinduism attracted the masses away from Buddhism; that there was some kind of self-destroying long-term degeneration in monastic community life. Certainly when Muslims settled in India, from the 8th century CE onwards, they were able without difficulty to eradicate what remained of Buddhism in India: by then the monasteries were vulnerable to the wholesale destruction they suffered at the hands of the Muslim iconoclasts.

While the Theravādins never attributed any kind of essence to dharmas as the Sarvāstivādins did, both schools of Abhidharmikas challenged the Nyāya-Vaiśeṣikas on how they understood the relation between the cognitive appearance of objects and their ontological status, as well as the status of qualities, universals and particulars, and so on. The Abhidharmika critique centred on the nature and prolific quantity of the atoms postulated by the Nyāya-Vaiśeṣikas. They stated that it was erroneous and superfluous to categorize so many factors as separate types of atoms: qualities and universals, for example, were part of the cognitive event – necessary to it, but not separate ontological categories. In their critique of the absolute independence and eternality of atoms, a key argument of the Abhidharmikas' centered on the impossibility of partless atoms becoming joined with one another to form the various objects of our experience. If partless, how can part of atom X abut or join with part of atom Y? Furthermore, they denied both the claim that perception established the external reality of what is perceived, and also that what was perceived was atoms inhering together to produce discrete 'particular' wholes. The latter claim, the Abhidharmikas pointed out, denied the possibility of ever perceiving parts as well as wholes. And in any case, what is perceived has only temporary phenomenological status. Nyāya-Vaiśeṣika literature contains responses to these and other critiques, and indicates the way in which they either revised or reinforced some of their doctrinal points accordingly.

Having inherited from the earliest stages of Buddhism teachings that were far from philosophically explicit, and which were in any case primarily concerned with their soteriological efficacy, the Abhidharmikas were working with two concurrent situations. One was their belief that the growing Buddhist tradition needed to establish for its practising members a more detailed and systematic presentation of the teachings, replacing doctrinal ambiguity with definitive interpretation. They did this by drawing on a range of technical criteria from linguistic analysis to meditative practices. The other was the developing tendency to present teachings systematically in order to establish the validity and coherence of these criteria for themselves, and also to enable them to engage more readily with the conflicting claims of outsiders on similar matters. To some extent the Abhidharmikas were more or less forced into some kind of system of analysis and categorization of dharmas in order to render their teachings comparable with the Nyāya-Vaiśeṣikas.

Emptiness and the Perfection of Wisdom

It is highly likely, therefore, that the character of the Abhidharmikas' work demonstrates the interacting of different schools of thought and how these sought to present their own views in a way that conformed to the presentation of others. While the Buddhists did offer criticisms of the Nyāya-Vaiśeṣika views, in fact what happened over time was that the dharmas of the Abhidharmikas became increasingly reified: what were originally understood in more or less abstract terms gradually acquired the status of plural and real 'things'. In the light of the non-realism of the earliest Buddhist teachings, this reification presented an open invitation to a serious critique of the Abhidharmikas' position. When this came, it was from within the Buddhist tradition, and it contributed to the emergence of what is called Mahāyāna Buddhism, a pan-Buddhist movement that sought to establish a less misleading definitive understanding of the Buddha's teachings than that of the Abhidharmikas. Early stages of this movement are represented in literature known as the 'Treatises on the Perfection of Wisdom' (the *Prajñāpāramitā Sūtras*). These texts homed in on the dharma theories of the Abhidharmikas and exposed them as contrary to the teaching that all things are dependently originated and therefore lacking any kind of essence. The Perfection of Wisdom writers acknowledged that their predecessors had correctly recognized the non-essential nature of human selfhood, but claimed that they had completely failed to understand the generic nature of the 'not-self' doctrine. The Perfection of Wisdom writers therefore claimed to have a 'higher' and 'more correct' insight or wisdom, and so claimed that their teachings represented the 'superior way', which is what Mahāyāna means.

When putting forward their critique of the Abhidharmikas, the

Perfection of Wisdom writers had an advantage over the Buddha: they were not operating in a milieu in which the dominant new teaching was the brahmins' claim that human beings have an essential self (ātman) that is identical with the essence of the universe (Brahman). These later Buddhists were therefore free to put forward their formulation of the Buddha's doctrine in terms which made no mention of self, but stated rather that all things (dharmas) are empty (*śūnya*) of 'own being' (svabhāva). The neutral term 'emptiness' made the teaching less open to subjective appropriation and its generic applicability more conceptually graspable.

Nārgārjuna's Middle Way

Not long after the Perfection of Wisdom material began to emerge, the most devastating critique of any kind of realism or pluralism was put forward by Nāgārjuna, a brilliant Buddhist thinker who lived during the 2nd century CE. Nāgārjuna's seminal work is the *Madhyamaka Kārikā* (MK), 'Writings on the Middle Way', which also gives its name to the Madhyamaka school of thought associated with him. It is clear from the opening verses of the MK that Nāgārjuna believed he was putting forward an interpretation of the Buddha's teachings rather than a philosophical view of his own. It is also clear that he believed the central import of the Buddha's teachings was to be found in the doctrine of dependent origination: it is this doctrine that encapsulates what is meant by the 'middle way'. Nāgārjuna explains that this tied in with the Perfection of Wisdom teachings because: 'It is dependent origination that we refer to as "emptiness"; it is this that is the middle way' (MK 24.18). That is (and one can see how this is a reiteration of the teachings of the Buddha as described in Chapter 3), what is dependently originated is 'empty' of 'self-essence' (i.e. independent existence).

Nāgārjuna's critique of pluralism is as applicable to the atoms of Nyāya-Vaiśeṣikas as to the ambiguous ontological status of the Abhidharmikas' categories of dharmas (particularly to those of the Sarvāstivādins, to which were attributed an essence or 'own being' – svabhāva). It is likely, however, that his primary aim was to rectify what he saw as the aberrations of the latter in their presentation of Buddhist teachings. Picking up on their concern with dharmas, he states that not only do dharmas not have any kind of 'own being', but it is also impossible that dharmas with 'own being' can come about. His critique begins with the radical statement: 'Nowhere and in no way do any entities exist which originate from themselves, from something else, from both, or spontaneously.' (MK 1.1). In this statement Nāgārjuna was neither stating nor seeking to show that nothing exists. Rather, his concern was to establish the ontological implications of dependent origination in order to understand correctly the status of what there is. He believed that terms such as 'being' (as in 'own being' – what in English we might also call 'entity' or 'thing') were being used in the sense of erroneously implying the independent existence of what they referred to, and that the idea of a law of causation operating between such entities – dependent origination wrongly understood – was fallacious. His critique was aimed at demonstrating these points.

What Nāgārjuna states here can be better understood in four stages as follows: (1) It is not the case that something with 'own being' is produced from itself. (2) Nor is it the case that something with 'own being' is produced from something other than itself. (3) Nor, indeed, could it be produced from both itself and the other. The underlying point of these stages is that it is illogical to think that anything with 'own being' can come about by means of causes or conditions, because any entity that is caused or conditioned would be contingent: 'contingent own being' is nonsensical, and there is no independently existing causal 'other' anyway. (This is reiterated in MK 15.1–3.) (4) The final stage is the impossibility of things with 'own being' arising spontaneously, because if this were the case the world would be one of random chaos, which it is not. Commentators on Nāgārjuna added the further explanations that if something produced itself this would result in a continuous unbreakable chain of production of the same thing; that it is impossible for something with a particular 'own being' to produce something with a completely different 'own being' – where could the causal connection lie?; and that a mixture of these two modes of production would suffer from both kinds of problem.

Dependent origination, then, is not a theory of causation with respect to bringing about a pluralistically real world. The world of which dependent origination is the operational factor is of a different ontological status: one of 'emptiness'. This cannot be understood in terms of existence or non-existence, because neither applies to it. Existence is not the case because the conceptual meaning of existence predicates a plurally real world. If such a world were the case it would be fixed and unchanging for ever more because, as Nāgārjuna has shown, no law of causation can operate in such a world: independent constituents cannot be causally contingent. Non-existence is not the case because by means of dependent origination we do experience the phenomenal world. Here Nāgārjuna introduces the notion of 'two truths', conventional and ultimate, relating respectively to the empirical world of experience and to things 'as they really are'.

Two Truths and the Logic of Emptiness

The empirical world of experience is not unreal: we really experience it. If one could but see it, however, from the point of view of 'things as they really are', or ultimate truth (and of course this is what following the Buddhist path is intended to achieve – Enlightenment), one would know that the nature of its reality – its ontological status – is not the independent pluralism it appears to us as. Rather, what we take to be independent pluralism is in fact a world of conditioning and dependence – which in ultimate terms is conventional – and therefore 'empty' of any kind of essence or 'own being'. It follows from this that the experiential world with which we are familiar, characterized by seemingly separate and substantively existing contents, is all part of the conventional level of truth: which is another reason why it is erroneous to seek to understand things as they really are (ultimate truth) in terms of any criteria relating to 'existence'. Misunderstanding this, and suggesting that emptiness means non-existence, Nāgārjuna says, is to miss the profound teaching of the Buddha and will destroy weak-minded people (MK 24.9–11). In fact, he goes on, emptiness is the only logical ontological possibility for the world of empirical existence: holding to pluralistic realism is particularly illogical because it precludes any causation and change.

Nāgārjuna's stance on emptiness is most often referred to by means of the fourfold formula (earlier found in material attributed to the Buddha himself, as discussed in Chapter 3) that it is erroneous to think of anything in terms of existence, non-existence, both existence and non-existence, or neither existence nor non-existence. Much has been written, by Buddhists and scholars alike, as to exactly how the logic of this should be understood, what its implications are, whether it leads inexorably to some kind of nihilism, or whether it should be taken solely as a critique of the positions of others, establishing no position of its own. For our purposes, I think it is most helpful to see it as a way of comprehensively rejecting any possible position of opponents on the fundamental grounds that a prerequisite of any ontological theory posited in terms of existence/non-existence is drawing on the conceptual framework of merely conventional truth. From the point of view of ultimate truth it thus cannot be true: the very stating of it being self-refuting. The best way forward, and what one should be aiming to achieve if one wants to understand the nature of reality, according to Nāgārjuna, is the 'calming of all verbal differentiation'. Whatever we verbalize about reality is bound to be false because of the falsity of the premises of the conventional world in which verbalization operates. One should, therefore, seek to gain insight that is not structured in such terms (this is the aim of meditative disciplines). From this, it follows that 'emptiness' is itself to be understood as conventional and not an independently existing transcendent entity of some non-verbal kind.

Emptiness affirms the world as we know it

To an objector who states that if everything is empty then nothing exists, and that in propounding emptiness Nāgārjuna is denying the existence of the Buddha and his teaching, Nāgārjuna replies:

> In suggesting this, you obviously do not understand emptiness, and are tormenting yourself unnecessarily about non-existence. One has to understand the nature of reality in terms of two truths, conventional and ultimate: this is the profound teaching of the Buddha, which will destroy those of weak intelligence who understand it wrongly. Only if emptiness is logical is the empirical world logical; without emptiness, the empirical world is absurd. If you state that entities are independently real then you deny the possibility of conditions and causal relationships. Nothing with which we are familiar could occur if all is not dependently originated [i.e. empty]: nothing could arise or cease, no knowledge could be acquired or ignorance eradicated, no activity undertaken, there could be no birth or death, everything would be immovable, without changing its state. It is you not I who suggest the non-existence of the world as we know it. If you deny emptiness you deny the world. But those who see the truth of dependent origination see the world as it really is, and understand the Buddha's teaching of dukkha, its arising, and the way to its cessation.
>
> (*Madhyamaka Kārikā* ch. 24 – paraphrase)

NB The last point identifies the sense of what Nāgārjuna is saying with the Buddha's Noble Truths.

Nāgārjuna writes of the 'emptiness of emptiness': it is a description not a substratum. Furthermore, there is no ontological difference between levels of truth: the only difference is experiential. For so long as one is ignorant of how things really are, one is subject to the experiences and criteria of conventional truth. When one gains insight, one sees the conventionality and understands emptiness. In complete contrast to the Vedic exegetes and the Nyāya-Vaiśeṣikas, what language predicates for Nāgārjuna is not a transcendentally pluralistic reality but a conventional world that has to be 'seen through' if one is to realize absolute truth.

The calming of verbal differentiation

> The very ideas of 'entity' and 'non-entity', 'existence' and 'non-existence', are part of a fallacious attitude towards the empirical world of conventional truth. Neither the positive nor the negative is therefore true. Nor is it possible that anything could be both one and the other at the same time since by any standards this is mutually contradictory. And for something to be 'neither one nor the other' is meaningful only if the initial premises are true, which in this case they are not. At neither level of truth is it correct to think of things as existing, non-existing, both, or neither: such conventions are erroneous at the conventional level and inapplicable at the ultimate level. Since all dharmas are empty, what can there be that is finite, infinite, both, or neither? what can there be that is eternal, temporal, both, or neither? Liberating insight comes with the calming of all such verbal differentiation. At no time did the Buddha teach anyone about 'things', only about verbal differentiation.
>
> (*Madhyamaka Kārikā* 11–24 – paraphrase)

Establishing Nāgārjuna's 'means of knowledge' is hazardous if one is to be true to his two levels of truth: all sensory and intellectual activity take place only conventionally, and therefore nothing that comes to us by means within this framework is reliable. But Nāgārjuna is adamant that the level of conventional truth is the realm in or from which insight is gained, and that its reality is meaningful according to its own criteria. In this context, one can see the importance for him of logic. But unlike the logical methodology of Nyāya, Nāgārjuna uses logic to undermine the fundamental premise on which all other extant means of knowledge rest: the external reality of the empirical world. Whether Nāgārjuna sought solely to reduce the viewpoints of everyone else to absurdity in this way, or whether he also used logic to establish a position of his own on emptiness, was an issue that divided his followers. Two distinct Madhyamaka schools of thought were established along these lines, and later critics, both within the Buddhist tradition and outside it, addressed both.

The Buddha's Enlightenment insights – a reminder

1. Seeing the continuity of his previous lives leading to the present.
2. Seeing other beings born and reborn in circumstances conditioned by their actions.
3. Seeing how to uproot the deepest of the binding continuity tendencies:

   i All sensory desires.
   ii The desire for continued existence.
   iii Ignorance.
   iv *Holding to viewpoints.* [my italics]

Mind-Only

An important non-Madhyamaka school of thought established some two centuries after Nāgārjuna was the Citta-Mātra ('Mind Only') or Yogācāra ('Practice of Yoga') school. Associated in its early stages with two brothers named Asaṅga and Vasubandhu, who lived during the 4th century CE, its approach also sought to rectify the Abhidharma reification of dharmas, but differed from Madhyamaka in two obvious ways. First, it focused specifically on the analysing of mental processes; second, it was concerned to present Buddhism in what it saw as a less negative light. The teaching on emptiness propounded by Perfection of Wisdom and Madhyamaka thinkers was thought by some to have unattractive and potentially misleading nihilistic connotations, directing attention away from the actual practice of understanding meditative states in order to attain liberating insight.

The Yogācāra approach, as evidenced in Vasubandhu's *Viṃśatikā* and *Triṃśikā* treatises, was to analyse the different types of 'state of mind', or 'consciousness event', which constitute one's pre-Enlightenment experiential world. Questions they addressed included What is it about those states of mind that bring about continuity? How does the karmic process of experiencing consequences of one's actions work? What is it that makes us ignorant? What has to happen in order for one to 'see things as they really are'?

The underlying problem, we are told, is that the commonly experienced world of self and other, subject and object, 'grasper' and 'grasped', is a mental construction, created by 'transformations of consciousness', imposed on a reality which, as it really is, is not like that. Continuity operates because transformations of consciousness as it were deposit 'seeds' in a 'consciousness storehouse', which come to fruition at some future time, when they produce the then correlatedly conditioned mental construction. While unenlightened, the experience of this process has the subject – object structure with which we are familiar, the structure operating because the consciousness storehouse is 'defiled' by ignorance as to the true nature of reality. These defilements, which are of many kinds, construct the various characteristics of our common experience as well as those that are specific to an individual because of the fruition of his or her karmic 'seeds'.

In order to overcome continuity, and as it were exhaust the consciousness storehouse's fuel, one has to penetrate the conventionality of the subject – object structure of mental processes. This is done by meditative disciplines (*yogācāra*), and by understanding that experience has 'three aspects'. The one with which we are most familiar is the 'constructed' aspect: the mentally constructed subjective – objective world. At this level, the main feature is one of reification: the 'constructedly real' world. The 'dependent' aspect is the underlying mental activity which is as it were transformed, the 'raw data' of experience. This aspect cannot be denied: experience is the common

Vasubandhu's three aspects of experience

1 *The constructed aspect*: the everyday world of subjectivity and objectivity, which is superimposed by our mental activities on to reality, which is not itself like that; it is our own mental processes that interpret the superimposed construction as reality itself.

2 *The dependent aspect*: the underlying 'raw data' of subjective – objective experience; that which undergoes mental transformations and becomes the constructed aspect.

3 *The perfected aspect*: the flow of experiential data unaffected by mental transformations. This constitutes insight into reality as it really is: without any subject – object construction.

ground or given for all human beings that no amount of philosophical argument can refute. The 'perfected' aspect is the complete absence of any mental constructions operating on the experiential 'flow'.

Several features of this explanation are important to note. First, in explaining how the world of objectivity arises by means of transformations of consciousness, it denies claims by Nyāya-Vaiśeṣikas and others that perception of an object establishes the transcendental existence of that object. Second, it relates to the fact of experiential continuity in a 'positive' and psychologically appealing way: in insisting on the reality of experience its starting point is familiar rather than abstract. This was important in the psychologically baffling (and to some unacceptable) context of the doctrine of 'emptiness' as radically presented by Madhyamaka. Third, from an ontological point of view it is open to interpretation either abstractly or substantively. That is to say, karmic 'seeds' and 'consciousness storehouse' can be understood either as metaphors or as actual entities, as can the whole notion of 'mind-only'. Liberating insight might simply involve the cessation of the mental activities which, for so long as they continue, are metaphorically indicated by the expression 'consciousness storehouse' – as a kind of operation-in-progress; or it might mean that an actual 'consciousness storehouse' entity becomes purified, and has some continuing purified existence. Similarly, the 'transformation of consciousness' might mean the dynamics of mental activities which each person experiences, of a wholly non-concrete kind, or it might refer to the way consciousness as some kind of 'mind-stuff' is transformed into the world of experience in a more substantive sense, as a real substratum. The term 'mind-only' is appropriate to both approaches: the need to understand one's mental activities in order to attain liberating insight, and the claim that the experiential world consists of mind-stuff.

Yogācāra Buddhists themselves as well as scholars of Buddhism have been divided on this last issue. Within the tradition, the different approaches led to the establishing of different schools of Yogācāra

Buddhism. Scholars differ as to whether the tradition was always idealistic in the ontological sense (there is only mind-stuff), or whether it began as an investigation of mental activities, leaving ontological issues aside, and developed an idealistic school later. The early material is ambiguous, open to interpretation in either way reasonably convincingly. It is worth noting, however, that if Vasubandhu was suggesting a non-ontological investigation of subjective cognitive processes, he would have had much in common with both the teachings of early Buddhism and, though very differently presented, with Nāgārjuna's calming of verbal differentiation. Conversely, if he was seeking to establish an idealistic ontology, this would constitute a major change of direction.

Idealism

Idealism as an ontology holds that 'all there is is mind'. Some kind of 'mind-stuff' constitutes the underlying substratum of reality. It is in some manner 'transformed' by mental activities. Thus, what we see is not what there really is, because what we see is reified into objects of varying degrees of density: we are not aware of just 'mind-stuff'. Because there really is 'mind-stuff', idealism is not the same as saying 'there is nothing'. For this reason it is potentially misleading to describe it in terms of 'illusion'. Idealism is the antithesis of any kind of pluralistic realism. The latter affirms that the plurality of what we see is transcendentally real; the former denies that this is the case.

Vasubandhu and his followers in the Yogācāra tradition made a great contribution to the period in which Buddhist discourse flowered. Beginning with Nāgārjuna, for some centuries Buddhist thinkers offered some of the most original and sophisticated ideas and critiques in the Indian milieu. In particular, they offered a serious challenge to those who attributed realism to the world as it is appears to us by means of

Developments in Buddhist Thought

The **Buddha** taught: 'all dharmas are "not-self"; there is a regularity to things: everything is dependently originated.'

The **Abhidharmikas** attempted to understand more about the nature of reality in terms of dharmas.

The **Theravādin Abhidharmikas** categorized dharmas into 28 'physical' and 52 'mental' kinds, plus consciousness. It was intended that this should help in analyzing them during meditation.

The **Sarvāstivādin Abhidharmikas** stated that all dharmas exist through past, present, and future states. In this sense, they have some kind of momentary essence, or 'own-being'.

Over time, the dharmas of the **Abhidharmikas** became reified: they acquired a real and enduring status as 'things'.

The **Perfection of Wisdom** writers reiterated that all things are non-essential. They presented the 'not-self' doctrine by stating that all things are 'empty' of 'own-being'.

Nāgārjuna stated not only that all things are 'empty', but also that it is not possible for any independent entity to arise or occur in any way whatsoever. 'Emptiness' is thus another way of referring to dependent origination. Furthermore, the world as we know it is underpinned only by dependent origination: to deny this is to deny the world.

Yogācāra thought sought to present the metaphysics of emptiness in terms of the mental processes that 'construct' to the world as we know it.

sense perceptions, and to the independent existence of selves as perceivers. Rather, Buddhists were prepared to follow the logical implications of beginning with questioning the reliability of the cognitive process as a means of certain knowledge, however radical the results. Apart from his highly sophisticated and original writing on emptiness, in defence of what he saw as the true teaching of the Buddha, what Nāgārjuna established for Buddhism was the strength of logical argument in backing its position and its critiques of others. This led to a flourishing tradition of so-called 'Buddhist logic', in which logical arguments and refutations concerning dharmas and the nature of existence were engaged in with others at a highly intellectually specialized and technical level. Major Buddhist logicians included Diṅnāga and the outstandingly brilliant Dharmakīrti, who established rules of logical argument in debate with the later Naiyāyikas and others. While the 'givens' and aims might be radically opposed between the Buddhists and the realists, their respective arguments were of mutual meaning and interest because each followed the rules laid down between them.

Chapter 7
The Witness and the Watched: Yoga and Sāṃkhya

Yoga: Harmony and Control

From a very early stage in the Indian tradition, people were practising various kinds of mental exercises, or meditative disciplines, often known by the generic term 'yoga'. The earliest Brahmanical references to yoga are to be found in the Upaniṣads, but there is little doubt that these reflect a practice that even then had been developed over a considerable period. Over time, a great many different kinds of yoga have been taught, but they share an underlying rationale. 'Yoga' comes from the Sanskrit verbal root *yuj*, meaning 'to yoke' – in the sense of yoking one thing to another. The point for many lay in the idea of 'merging' or 'uniting': either self/soul (ātman) with universal essence (Brahman), or, in theistic systems, soul with God. It can also lie more in the linked concepts of internal 'control', 'harmony', 'order', or of what one might call 'integrity of insight'. The overall ontology can vary from system to system, but the common underlying principle was that normal life is characterized by 'being led astray' by our senses, and by the misleading busy-ness of everyday cognitive activity. The practice of yoga, therefore, is for the purpose of attaining control, calm, and, in some systems, cognitive insight.

The darśana of Classical Yoga is represented in a text known as the *Yoga Sūtras*. Commonly attributed to a man named Patañjali, in fact the

Chronology

c.2000 BCE*–* : the Vedic sacrificial tradition.

c.800–500 BCE: the early Upaniṣads.

by 500 BCE: ritual and gnostic branches of the Brahmanical tradition coexisted.

5th-century BCE *milieu*: householders and renouncers.

c.485–405 BCE: the lifetime of the Buddha.

4th–2nd century BCE: grammarians and early exegetes establish the criteria of what should be 'looked at'.

3rd–2nd century BCE: Vaiśeṣika and Nyāya combine an ontology of pluralistic realism and a formal method by which to arrive at certain knowledge.

4th–1st century BCE: emergence of different Buddhist schools

3rd century BCE*–2nd century* CE: development of the Buddhist Abhidharma.

1st century BCE*–1st century* CE: the emerging of Mahāyāna Buddhism and the early *Prajñāpāramitā* ('Perfection of Wisdom') *Sūtras*.

c.2nd century CE: Nāgārjuna's *Madhyamaka Kārikā* focus on the 'emptiness' (śūnyatā) of all phenomena.

c.4th century CE: the Cittamātra/Yogācāra school of Buddhism centres on mental processes.

3rd century CE: The *Yoga-Sūtras* represent what is known as 'Classical Yoga'. Said to have been written by one Patañjali, in fact their authorship is uncertain. The *Yoga-Sūtras* present a detailed mental disciplinary methodology for attaining liberating insight, a methodology that is compatible with the ontology of Sāṃkhya.

4th – 5th century CE: Īśvarakṛṣṇa codifies classical Sāṃkhya in his *Sāṃkhya Kārikā*. Human beings are bound to rebirth because they do not realize that what they take to be conscious is unconscious, and that consciousness lies only in ontologically separate and inactive 'selves' (*puruṣa*). The aim is to gain insight into this dualism.

authorship of the *Yoga Sūtras* is not known, and there were in any case several Patañjalis (including the grammarian mentioned in Chapter 4). The text incorporates a comprehensive yoga methodology. Indeed, it seems that the method is its main purpose, with references to the ontology to which it adheres being included only in order to justify or elaborate the purpose and structure of the methodology. While concerned with similar issues and similar details, virtually no references are made to other systems of thought: if the proponents of Classical Yoga engaged in debate with others, those encounters are not recorded here. The text is above all a manual for practice, and its various criteria and formulations were undoubtedly arrived at from within a long tradition of practice as opposed to debate. Philosophical abstractions are of less interest to the yogic practitioner than the insights of meditation, and efficacy in practice of more importance than convincing others. This darśana perhaps exemplifies more than any other that Indian 'philosophy' is part of a tradition whose primary aim and purpose was soteriological.

The Purpose of Classical Yoga

The *Yoga-Sūtras* open by stating their aim:

> Now the explanation of yoga: yoga is the cessation of the activities of the mind (*citta-vṛtti-nirodha*: mind-activity-cessation). (Yoga Sūtra 1.1–2)

The activities of the mind (*citta-vṛtti*) are of many different kinds, under the broad headings of valid cognitions, misconceptions, conceptualizations, sleep, and memory. The means of knowledge for valid cognitions are sense-perception, inference, and the testimony of tradition. Misconceptions are invalid cognitions, not based on any actual reality. Conceptualizations are cognitions based merely on abstract mental activities – the tendency to conceptualize reality only in terms of 'the reifying of verbiage', one might say. This actively interferes with seeing reality as it really is. Sleep also involves its own kind of mental activity, and memory is the carrying around with us of whatever we have experienced, involving more mental activity. The cessation of all of these is achieved by means of yogic practice and detachment (i.e. control). Experiences and states of mind such as sickness, doubt, carelessness, sloth, falseness, failure, and instability all distract consciousness and constitute obstacles to achieving cessation. Pain, depression, trembling of the limbs, and poor breathing accompany these obstacles. The way out lies in focusing the mind single-pointedly, practising outward-lookingness (i.e. not being self-centred in the selfish sense), benevolence towards others, right breathing, and mental steadiness. (This explanation is paraphrased from *Yoga Sūtra* 1.5–22, 29–35.)

From this can be seen that the author of the text denies that ultimate reality is arranged in the way we conceive of it according to our experience of the manifest world. Mental activities in general create distractions which seriously distort and lead us away from clear perception of reality. Underpinning the Yoga methodology is the aim to discriminate that the true 'seer' or 'self', known in this system as *puruṣa*, is absolutely separate from the 'seen' or 'manifest', *prakṛti*. Until discrimination is achieved, each individual wrongly believes that the 'seer', which is where consciousness lies, is part of what is manifest. We confuse our manifest, unconscious 'ego' with our 'higher self', when in fact the latter is wholly other: the manifest world is one of unconscious activity; consciousness belongs to puruṣas, which are also inactive. It is the 'conjunction' of puruṣa and prakṛti that brings about the delusion: discrimination, achieved when the distracting activities of the mind are stilled, effects their disassociation. Thus is the true self liberated from bondage to rebirth, which continues for so long as there is conjunction. It is the true self (puruṣa) that is of the highest and 'truest' reality; realizing it is the *summum bonum* to which human beings can aspire. Knowledge of the true nature of the self, and the reality of one's essential puruṣa, is the central concern of the *Yoga Sūtras*. In spite of our ignorance as to where consciousness lies, in Classical Yoga the manifest world is not unreal. Prakṛti – the manifest world – is ontologically existent in its own right, as are puruṣas. But prakṛti is a world both of distraction from the true and 'higher' state of things and of bondage to rebirth. The aim, therefore, is to discriminate selfhood from prakṛti.

Īśvara – the 'Lord' – in Classical Yoga

In Yoga Sūtra 1.23–8, we are told that the goal of discrimination can also be achieved by means of 'devotion to the Lord (Īśvara)'. The Lord is said to be 'a special puruṣa', untouched by karmic activities, all-knowing, and teacher of ancient sages. Exactly what these verses mean is not obvious, and there has been disagreement among scholars as to the status of this Lord: whether it/he is a transcendent being, giving Classical Yoga a theistic aspect; whether these verses refer to the fact that the methodology of Classical Yoga was followed by adherents of theistic sects; whether Īśvara is an abstract archetype; or whether the verses are metaphorically indicating what each individual will find if they 'look within': each person's puruṣa is his or her own 'Lord'. In Indian religious traditions devotion can sometimes mean 'single-mindedness' rather than 'worship'; thus the expression here does not necessarily imply devotion to an actual deity.

The practice of yoga by the deluded individual is necessary for two reasons. First, ignorance occurs only at the manifest level. Second, it is at the manifest level that discrimination takes place. Being inactive, puruṣa does, and can do, nothing: its role is that of witness.

The bulk of the *Yoga Sūtras* comprises descriptive information about different states of mind, different ways of controlling mental activities, different levels of attainment, what contributes to the cessation of the activities of the mind and what does not, and so on. Some of this concerns the way in which selfhood is experienced, both as the false prakṛti-level 'ego' and as the discriminated puruṣa. Much of it is, in its own context, technical, and has little actual meaning to those who have no experience of meditative states. One Western scholar of Classical Yoga has described the material as 'primarily practical maps for the process of an interior journey', which graphically suggests that the text principally represents not a clear philosophical or ontological stance, but an account of meditative practices by means of which all activities of the mind that hinder discrimination are controlled.

Sāṃkhya: Reasoning for Dualism

By contrast, the main text of Classical Sāṃkhya more overtly incorporates an elaborately explained ontology and clear discussion of its means of knowledge. This text, the *Sāṃkhya Kārikā* (SK), is said to have been written by Īśvarakṛṣṇa between 350 and 450 CE. It is clear from evidence in a variety of sources that there had been a long earlier history of Sāṃkhya thought, going back to Upaniṣadic times, which might well have differed in detail and from time to time in comparison with what is now taken as the tradition's key text. No earlier Sāṃkhya text survives, however.

The Sanskrit term *sāṃkhya* has several meanings, but in the context of this tradition means something like 'enumeration'. It refers to the point that the truth that the school purports to teach is known by means of enumerating, in the sense of analysing and discriminating, the categories which constitute the manifest world. The SK opens by stating: 'It is because of the anguish of suffering that the desire arises to know how to overcome it.' Following this clearly stated soteriological purpose, it goes on to state that what is required is a special kind of discriminative knowledge, which can discern 'the manifest, the unmanifest, and the knower'. The next verses establish the ontological distinction between puruṣas (the knowers – which are numerically plural, individually discrete, but ontologically identical to each other) and prakṛti (both manifest and unmanifest – but numerically one). Sāṃkhya, like Classical Yoga, is ontologically dualistic in this way: reality is comprised of puruṣas and prakṛti. In its unmanifest state, prakṛti is an uncreated ontological 'given', becoming manifest (its 'created' form) when in conjunction with a puruṣa (how this happens is unexplained). An important point in support of Sāṃkhya's dualism is that what becomes manifest is said to have pre-existed in unmanifest prakṛti: nothing new is created. This view, which we shall see again in the next chapter, is referred to by the term *satkāryavāda*: the view that the effect pre-exists in the cause. In the SK the point establishes both that the manifest world is ontologically really existent and that it is ontologically only one. The reasons given for satkārya in verse 9 are:

> Because non-being is non-productive;
> because a material cause is necessary;
> because things cannot arise haphazardly from different things;
> because things can only be produced from what is capable of producing them;
> because this is the nature of causation.

This verse exemplifies the importance to Sāṃkhya of inference as a means of knowledge. Another example is the inference that there must be a plurality of puruṣas 'because there is a diversity of births, deaths, and activities; because different things happen at different times; because people have differently proportioned characteristics' (SK v. 18).

The other means of knowledge it accepts are perception and reliable testimony. Perception is qualified as 'the selective ascertainment of particular sense objects' (SK v. 5), which means that not all 'ordinary' perception is valid. And reliable testimony relates to the tradition's heritage of specialization, going back to the Upaniṣads as primary source. Inference and perception, however, take precedence over reliable testimony, and where the latter is illogical the former prevail. An example of this can be seen in the use of inference to establish the plurality of puruṣas, rather than accepting as a given the Upaniṣadic suggestion that self (ātman) is one with the universal essence (Brahman).

Sāṃkhya's structure of reality

	prakṛti			
	unmanifest/	*buddhi*	*ahaṃkāra*	mind
puruṣa	manifest	(discriminator)	(I-maker)	5 sense organs
	(*sattva*/			5 action organs
	rajas/			5 subtle elements
	tamas)			5 gross elements

puruṣas are ontologically identical but numerically plural; they are eternal, unchanging, inactive, conscious witnesses

prakṛti is ontologically distinct from puruṣas; it is eternal, changing, active, unconscious

prakṛti is characterized by three qualities: goodness, energy or passion, and inertia, which combine in various proportions in all of the manifest world.

Qualities, Categories, and Discernment

The whole of prakṛti is 'coloured' by three fundamental qualities, the 'characteristics' of SK v. 18, loosely translated from the Sanskrit as goodness, energy or passion, and inertia. The variously proportioned combinations of these three in any given being or object serve to 'manifest, activate, and limit; to successively dominate, support, and interact with one another' (SK v. 12), thus explaining how there are different categories or species, and differences between people and things of the same kind. For liberating discrimination to take place, there must be no imbalance of the qualities.

As well as this threefold nature of prakṛti, its manifestation is structured according to the various categories that require analytical discernment in order to overcome suffering. The first category is *buddhi*, which acts both as the 'will' of the individual and as the discriminating faculty: it is this which will 'selectively ascertain particular sense objects' in the quest for liberation, and eventually discriminate puruṣa. Next is *ahaṃkāra*, which literally means 'I-maker'. This is the ego, that in its ignorance of puruṣa mistakenly thinks it is the conscious self of the individual. After these two major categories comes mind, as a category in its own right, followed by a series of 'sets': the sense organs (eye, ear, nose, tongue, skin); the action organs (voice, hands, feet, excretory organs, reproductive organs); the 'subtle elements' (sound, touch, form, taste, smell); and the 'gross elements' (space, wind, fire, water, earth).

The 'enumeration' (*sāṃkhya*) of these categories provides a picture both of how it is that human beings, constituted of unconscious prakṛti, think they are conscious, and also of how discrimination occurs from within that unconscious state. The I-maker is the constituent that makes us think we are conscious: it is phenomenologically experienced as the thinker of thoughts, the agent of deeds, the individual subject in the empirical world. It is, however, enveloped in prakṛti, which acts as it were as a blinker as to the true state of affairs. Buddhi, the individual's will and discriminatory faculty, is drawn towards the powerful I-maker as the focus of the individual's experiential life, which is altogether away from the ever-present but inactive puruṣa. It takes the combined efforts of the individual's faculties (and this would be thought to be over many lifetimes) to reorient the direction of buddhi's discriminatory activities. The *Sāṃkhya Kārikā* states many times that the innate purpose of the entire structure is to seek to discriminate puruṣa. But this involves overcoming the pull and distractions caused by out-of-balance qualities, in particular by a predominance of either passion or inertia. These bring about all manner of ignorances, inadequacies, attachments, and complacencies. Eventually, however, it is possible for the individual's buddhi to extricate itself from involvement with the vicissitudes of cyclical life sufficiently to perceive that what the I-maker creates is merely a false or inferior self, and that the true self is puruṣa, detached and silently waiting in the wings. This perception effects disassociation of puruṣa from prakṛti and liberates the individual from rebirth.

So qualitatively inferior is prakṛti to puruṣa, and so deluded is the sense of self imparted by the I-maker, that it is stated in the *Sāṃkhya Kārikā* that in fact 'nothing really is bound; no-one is reborn and no-one is released' (SK v. 62). As it is only prakṛti that is involved in cyclical experience, and as the conscious 'selves' of prakṛti are a delusion, in fact rebirth of such 'individuals' does not constitute rebirth of real selves. Puruṣas merely witness.

No detailed methodology is given in the *Sāṃkhya Kārikā* for achieving discrimination. There is mention of the need to practise proper reasoning and study, and to obtain good instruction, as well as to perfect ethical qualities (SK v. 51). Otherwise, the system provides a structure compatible with the practice of the meditative exercises of Classical Yoga. The different terminology of Sāṃkhya's distracting delusions could without difficulty be seen in terms of the 'activities of the mind' of the *Yoga Sūtras*.

A Postscript on Prakṛti

What invites questioning is whether the manifestation of prakṛti as described in the *Sāṃkhya Kārikā* can legitimately be understood as the manifestation of a real and plural world, as it is most often taken to be. I have chosen not to translate prakṛti in this book, but common translations are 'nature' and 'matter' (presumably in contrast to puruṣa as 'soul' or 'consciousness'). The categories of manifestation include all the gross elements that are normally associated with matter, and omit nothing that one might associate with the empirical world about us. But the order in which the manifestation occurs is the opposite of what one might expect if it is the empirical world, peopled by individuals in a real and plural sense, that is being described. In the text, cognitive faculties come first. And it is from the I-maker that the characteristics of the natural world subsequently emerge. Furthermore, the three qualities of which the whole thing is comprised - goodness, energy or passion, and inertia - are qualities that might well be considered psychological rather than material. One wonders, therefore, whether what is being described is a cognition-dependent world - each individual's own 'world of experience' - as described in the context of early Buddhist teachings in Chapter 3. This interpretation of the *Sāṃkhya Kārikās* might be problematic in the context of Sāṃkhya's ontological dualism - certainly as dualism is conventionally understood, and also its satkārya viewpoint (effect pre-existing in the cause) - which in this context is usually understood in terms of the transformation of prakṛti as substance. But it would fit well with the human existential problem as stated, and with the text's soteriological aim. And its compatibility with Classical Yoga's method would be unaffected. It is possible that the origin of the text's ambiguity on this issue lies in the long earlier tradition of Sāṃkhya, about which little is known.

Chapter 8
The Word and the Book
Bhartṛhari, Mīmāṃsā, and Vedānta

From the 4th century BCE onwards, orthodox Brahmanical thinkers continued the traditions of grammatical and exegetical work on the Vedic corpus of material which had been established by figures such as Pāṇini and Patañjali, Jaimini, and Bādarāyaṇa. As the different strands of Indian thought developed, many sought to maintain the supremacy of strictly orthodox practices and worldviews – whether their primary concern was for the ritual and realism of the karma-kāṇḍa (action section) of the Veda, or for the knowledge and cosmic essentialism of the Upaniṣads, which constituted both the end of the Veda (vedānta) and its jñāna-kāṇḍa (knowledge section). It was not until the 5th century CE, however, that a significantly new and different grammatical approach was put forward, and yet later still that the most important branches of the Mīmāṃsā and Vedānta darśanas were established. Over time, both of the latter incorporated under their respective umbrellas some distinctive variations which were propounded by different important thinkers in their traditions, as well as the ideas of those key figures discussed below.

Bhartṛhari – Grammar Again

During the 5th century CE, the grammarian Bhartṛhari put forward the view that the understanding of the relationship between the classical language of Sanskrit and reality was not just a way of defending first

Chronology

c.*2000* BCE– : the Vedic sacrificial tradition.

c.*800–500* BCE: the early Upaniṣads.

by 500 BCE: ritual and gnostic branches of the Brahmanical tradition coexisted.

5th-century BCE *milieu*: householders and renouncers.

c.*485–405* BCE: the lifetime of the Buddha.

4th–2nd century BCE: grammarians and early exegetes.

3rd–2nd century BCE: Vaiśeṣika and Nyāya.

4th–1st century BCE: emergence of different Buddhist schools.

3rd century BCE–*2nd century* CE: development of the Buddhist Abhidharma.

1st century BCE–*1st century* CE: Mahāyāna Buddhism and the 'Perfection of Wisdom' Sūtras.

c.*2nd century* CE: Nāgārjuna's *Madhyamaka Kārikā.*

c.*4th century* CE: the Cittamātra/Yogācāra school of Buddhism.

3rd century CE: the *Yoga-Sūtras* of Classical Yoga.

4th–5th century CE: Īśvarakṛṣṇa codifies the dualistic ontology of classical Sāṃkhya.

5th century CE: the grammarian Bartṛhari develops an orthodox darśana alongside the philosophical activity of linguistic analysis. Understanding the role of language, he stated, leads to liberating knowledge of Brahman, the unifying essence of the universe.

7th century CE: the flowering of the Mīmāṃsā tradition of exegesis of the karma-kāṇḍa (action section) of the Vedas. Principal proponents include Kumārila and Prabhākara.

8th century CE: Śaṅkara's school of Advaita Vedānta, based on a 'non-dual' (advaita) exegesis of the Upaniṣads, 'the end of the Veda' and its jñāna-kāṇḍa (knowledge section).

11th century CE: Rāmānuja's Viśiṣṭādvaita Vedānta, a 'qualified non-dualism', also based on exegesis of the Upaniṣads.

principles – in his case the validity of the Veda and the world it represented – but was also a way of gaining liberating insight. In combining both these factors, Bhartṛhari saw grammar and the study of language as the highest of all religio-philosophical activities. His claim was that through understanding the way Sanskrit was correlated with the manifest world, by means of Vedic utterances, one could arrive at knowledge of the universal absolute (Brahman): language itself is, in a very real sense, the sound of reality.

> That which is one, divided in different ways by differences in construction: Brahman, that highest one, is known when one attains an understanding of grammar.
>
> (Bhartṛhari's *Vākyapadīya* 1.22)

Bhartṛhari was working at a time when a key concern of the grammarians was analysing the nature of the components of a sentence as the means by which knowledge is acquired. According to Bhartṛhari, it is a complete sentence that comprises a unit of meaning, the utterance of a sentence instantaneously conveying valid knowledge in a way individual words and phrases do not: the latter convey only partial and incomplete fragments of knowledge, which are both easily distorted and misleading. Furthermore, as meaning and words are united in the way we comprehend through sentences, there can be no knowledge except by means of language: to know something is to know it as it is expressed in language. So reality itself can be seen as knowable by means of comprehending its expression in sentences - or, rather, in one sentence. Bhartṛhari stated that while one can break down language into units of sentences and their constituent parts for the purpose of grammatical analysis, in fact language, as the sound of the universe, is itself continuous and indivisible. Here he draws out what he sees as the logical implication of the Vedic view that the universe is actively maintained by means of the ritually uttered sounds associated with the sacrifice. And he states that insight into this 'monistic sound' (*śabda-Brahman*) is the goal one should seek to attain.

Because Bhartṛhari's teachings sought to understand the way language corresponds to reality, they were of serious interest to Buddhist logicians, particularly Diṅnāga. The worldviews from which each approached the language/reality debate differed: Bhartṛhari's view incorporated the maintaining of the universe by means of Vedic ritual, whereas the Buddhists thought verbal construction perpetuated the world of ignorance and cyclical continuity. But the issue itself was the same for both sides, and what one might call his unifying of the sound-activity of Vedic ritual with the apparent monism of the Upaniṣads makes Bhartṛhari a significant figure within the Brahmanical tradition, which tended to separate the two strands of thought and practice. Though neither Mīmāṃsakas nor Vedāntins adopted his views entirely, both had points in common with him; and some later Mīmāṃsakas in particular were influenced by what Bhartṛhari had said about the ontological implications of the way language operated.

Mīmāṃsā: the Philosophy of the Ritual

For Mīmāṃsā thinkers such as Kumārila and Prabhākara, exegetes of the Vedic ritual texts rather than grammarians per se, the main point of their enterprise was the proper understanding of the nature of ritual, in particular the injunctions of the sacrifice. Indeed, for the orthodox it was a key aspect of their sva-dharma ('own-duty') that they should do this, for the study of the Veda is an intrinsic part of the structure for ensuring that it is handed on through the generations. Mīmāṃsakas accepted as a given the realistic plurality of the world around us in which the sacrifice was performed, and saw the sacrifice as the means for the maintaining of that world. More specifically, it was the means for maintaining Dharma – how things should be: this was the fundamental rationale of the sacrificial ritual injunctions. The injunctions themselves, being contained in texts representing eternal Truth, were seen as self-validating, an intrinsic part of the Dharma-package, so to speak.

In their attempt to understand the nature of the ritual more philosophically, later Mīmāṃsakas (following Jaimini) found the work of the orthodox grammarians to be of crucial relevance in the way language was linked to the nature of the world. They held that the uttering of a word indicates the existence of that which it designates. This assisted them as they sought to demonstrate the reality and nature of the plural world, which included a plurality of independent and autonomous 'selves' as performers of the sacrifice. They denied claims to monism put forward by early exegetes of the Upaniṣads by arguing that such claims failed to accommodate individual characteristics and idiosyncracies, ignorance, wickedness, and virtue; and they stated that Upaniṣadic injunctions to know one's self were for the purpose not of liberation but for the better performance of Vedic rituals. Similarly, they denied the Sāṃkhya position of inactive selves whose identity is 'lost' when conjoined with prakṛti: rather, the Mīmāṃsakas stated, the nature of selfhood is conscious agent (and therefore active ritualist). As Kumārila said in his *Ślokavārtika*: 'The injunction that one has a duty to understand the self does not have a goal of liberation. Such self-knowledge is clearly intended to motivate performance of ritual.'

Plurality and Realism: Another Take on Categories

The plurality and realism of the world was also argued for by Mīmāṃsakas by means of iterating the nature of its characteristics. This they did in a way similar to the analyses and categorizing of the Vaiśeṣikas, described in Chapter 5. The Mīmāṃsakas accepted five categories: substance, quality, action, universality, and absence. To the nine kinds of substance itemized by the Vaiśeṣikas (earth, water, fire, air, ether, space, time, self, and mind), they added darkness and sound. The relationship between substance and qualities and other categories was subject to analysis which resulted in what is called an 'identity in difference' position. Where categories coexist, such as with the colour red and the form rose, they are different only insofar as they each contribute to an identity. They cannot exist separately. Indeed, nothing perceivable is wholly different or wholly identical: rather, things are distinct in relation to each other or identical while being of different categories. All cognition involves this 'identity in difference' of the various aspects of the combination of categories involved.

The Mīmāṃsakas' epistemological theory

For Mīmāṃsakas, cognition represented a fundamentally valid and reliable means of knowledge, both of the world around us and of individual 'selves' as knowers. The act of knowing 'reveals' the external 'transcendentally real' existence of both known and knower: neither of these, that is to say, is in any way dependent on the operating of the cognitive process. Rather, cognition brings about a state of 'being known' in the object of knowledge, and a confirmation of the existence of the autonomous knower. The process of knowing therefore reveals 'truth', and in this case confirms the worldview of the eternal Veda.

The Mīmāṃsakas also held to a theory that all substance is reducible to atomic particles. But in contrast to the Vaiśeṣikas' microscopic atoms, which are not individually perceivable and known to exist only by means of inference, the Mīmāṃsakas gave greater priority to the reliability of perception, and held that atoms are no smaller than what can be seen with the naked eye – such as a mote in a sunbeam. They thus held to a strong common-sense view of reality, a feature which is emphasized by their acceptance of cognition itself as a valid and intrinsically reliable means of knowledge of a world that is external and independent of that cognition. What is known exists, and cognitions should be understood as actions which produce the quality of being known in their objects. Acts of knowing thus reveal the reality of the plural world simply by virtue of their occurring.

The Veda is True

This epistemological theory requires not that cognition needs validating – as was the approach of others, most notably the Buddhists – but that it needs to be proved false by an opponent if subject to challenge. This put the Mīmāṃsakas in a strong position with regard to the validity of the Vedas and the ritual injunctions they sought to defend. The status of the performers of the sacrifice was similarly established in that the act of knowing was said to indicate the existence of the eternal self as knower of the empirical world. That is to say, it is not just that cognizing an implement of the sacrifice reveals the independent existence of that implement, but also that such a cognition reveals the existence of the cognizer: the cognition 'I know X' is the means by which both X and the self are known to have autonomous existence.

These last two related points – the establishing of self and world by means of cognition – were of primary importance to the Mīmāṃsakas because of their belief that the Veda was eternal truth manifested in language. They held to the orthodox view that the Veda had no author.

Rather, it is self-existent truth, and cognizing it is an act of revealing its validity because cognition is intrinsically absolutely reliable. In common with the nature of the Veda as a body of injunctions to act, so knowing is itself a revelatory activity – and the self, as knower, is related to the external world, as known, by means of such cognitive actions. As well as establishing the validity of the Veda, this position sought to privilege the knower of the Veda as the agent of the perpetuating of reality – a claim that had always been crucial to the orthodox tradition.

Śaṅkara's Non-dualism

Other orthodox thinkers, following the approach of Bādarāyaṇa and drawing on his summary of the Upaniṣads in the *Brahma Sūtra*, saw the injunctions of the Veda in the context of the need to acquire knowledge of the essence of the cosmos, Brahman, rather than the performing of sacrificial rituals. There is evidence of a long lineage of so-called 'Vedāntin' thinkers (the Upaniṣads are the vedānta, or 'end of the Veda'). But it was the highly influential Śaṅkara, who lived during the 8th century CE, who consolidated Vedānta thought systematically enough to engage in serious polemical debate with others. Śaṅkara's principal work was a commentary on Bādarāyaṇa's *Brahma Sūtra*, explicating what he saw as a definitive exegesis of the message of the Upaniṣads. His main non-commentarial work is the *Upadeṣa-Sāhasrī*, 'The Thousand Teachings'. Śaṅkara used the *Brahma Sūtra*, the Upaniṣads themselves, and the *Bhagavad Gītā* as his three basic texts, and his exegetical work sought to present their teaching as a unity – what is called the 'triple foundation' of revealed truth.

To grasp Śaṅkara's position of Advaita Vedānta, a 'non-dual' interpretation of the ontology principally expressed in the Upaniṣads, one might take his starting point as the passage from the *Chāndogya Upaniṣad* which states:

> In the beginning, this world was just Being [i.e. Brahman] – one only,

without a second. . . . And it thought to itself 'Let me become many; let me multiply myself.'

(*Chāndogya Upaniṣad* 6.2.1–3)

coupled with:

By means of just one lump of clay, everything made of clay can be known: any modifications are merely verbal distinctions, names; the reality is just clay.

(*Chāndogya Upaniṣad* 6.1.4)

These key passages establish for Śaṅkara two fundamental points: a non-dual, monistic universe, the substance of which is Brahman; and the fact that all change is only apparent – Brahman does not actually change. This kind of monism is a form of 'effect pre-existing in the cause' (*satkāryavāda*) different from that we saw in the context of Sāṃkhya in Chapter 7. Here, the effect does not involve any actual transformation of the material cause, but is just an apparent manifestation of plurality. This is called *vivarta-vāda*: '[manifestation] by way of appearance'.

Śaṅkara goes to some lengths, however, to establish that the appearance of plurality does have conventional reality even if it is not ultimately real. He introduces two 'levels of reality' – conventional and absolute – in the process exposing himself to accusations of being a 'crypto-Buddhist'. Śaṅkara emphatically denied such claims, denouncing the emptiness and non-essentiality of Buddhist teachings, and proclaiming the fundamental reality of Brahman, the Being of the *Chāndogya Upaniṣad*, as the material substance of the universe. It is knowledge of the existent Brahman that is the ultimate experiential goal for man, not (merely) knowledge of the unsubstantiality of the cognitively constructed empirical realm, he said.

Śaṅkara also strongly criticized Sāṃkhya dualism as false, and stated that the plural realism of the Naiyāyikas and Mīmāṃsakas was to

Śaṅkara's non-dualism

The *advaita* of Śaṅkara's Advaita Vedānta denotes an interpretation of the Upaniṣads that gives a 'non-dual', or monistic, ontology. Everything is Brahman. It follows from this that one's self, ātman, is also Brahman: hence the famous expression 'ātman is Brahman'. For Śaṅkara, Brahman is an unchanging absolute essence. All plurality is only apparent, not actual. This does not mean, however, that it is correct to state that the plurality of the empirical world is absolutely unreal or non-existent. Rather, it is of only 'conventional' reality. His most frequently cited analogy is of seeing a snake where there is in fact a coiled rope. The false sighting is 'real' to us when it takes place, and has 'real' effects on us. But the coiled rope has remained unchanged, and can be perceived for what it 'more really' is when the false perception is seen through. Another related analogy more specifically relating to the self as a part of unchanging Brahman is:

> . . . The notion that the self undergoes rebirth and change is similar to the [false] experience one has when moving along a river in a boat that the trees on the banks are moving. Just as the trees seem to be moving in the opposite direction to the person in the boat, so the self seems to be being reborn.
>
> (*Upadeśa-Sāhasrī* 5.2–3)

mistake conventional plurality for absolute reality. Furthermore, all of these erroneous positions are in conflict with the true (i.e. Śaṅkara's) interpretation of the Upaniṣads; and whatever arguments, logical or otherwise, others might put forward in support of their stance, they all become invalid in the face of that Upaniṣadic interpretation.

In support of Śaṅkara's non-dualism

> The self (ātman), indeed, is this whole world.
>
> (*Chāndogya Upaniṣad* 7.25.2)
>
> Brahman, indeed, is this whole world, this widest extent.
>
> (*Muṇḍaka Upaniṣad* 2.2.11)
>
> One should not on the strength of mere logic challenge something that has to be ascertained from the Vedas.
>
> (*Śaṅkara's Brahma Sūtra Bhāṣya* 2.1.11)

The experience of conventional reality for Śaṅkara is one which arises because of ignorance as to the true nature of absolute reality. It is not unchanging Brahman but ignorance that is the source and cause of empirical plurality. And the overcoming of ignorance and the gaining of knowledge of the identity of one's essential self (ātman) and the universal essence (Brahman) effects liberation from the ignorance-induced cycle of rebirth. To the question 'where does ignorance come from if everything is Brahman?', Śaṅkara replies that from the standpoint of knowledge, there is no ignorance to ask the origin of: knowledge as it were 'cancels' all thinking in terms of ignorance; and from the standpoint of ignorance, the question cannot be answered as the notion of the beginning of ignorance is asked and meaningful only from within ignorance itself.

The conventional world is of crucial importance to Śaṅkara for two key reasons. First, it is at that level that the Veda reveals eternal truth. And second, it is at that level that one can seek to gain liberating insight. In a similar but more practically illustrative vein to Śaṅkara's rope-and-snake and bank-of-river analogies (see box on page 127), modern Advaita Vedāntins explain as follows: You are dreaming that you are

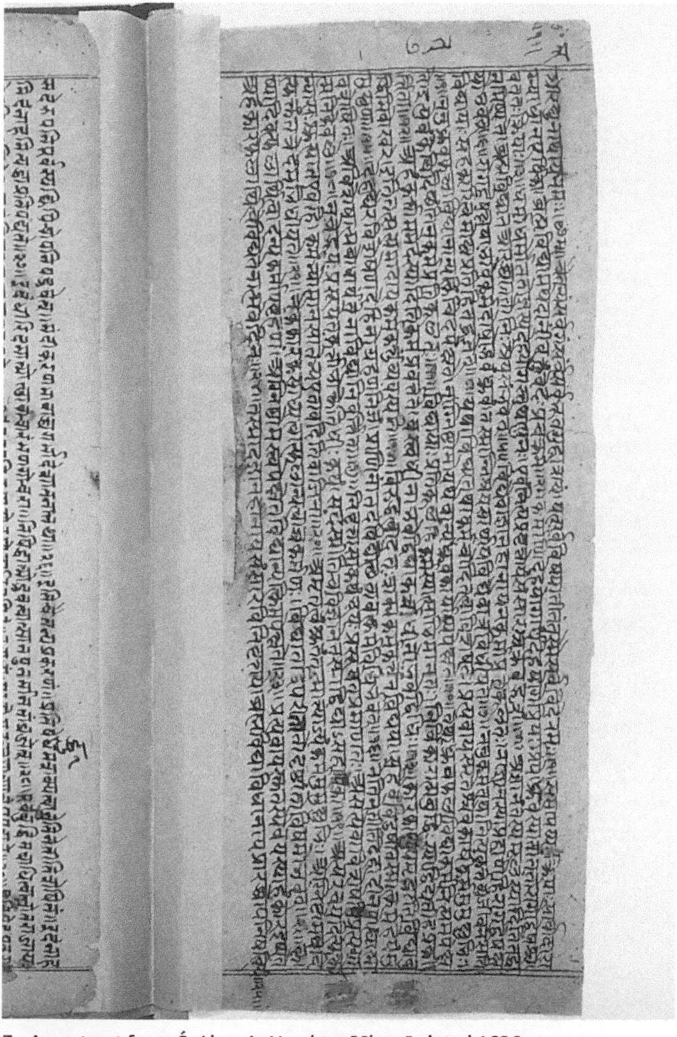

7. An extract from Śaṅkara's *Upadeṣa-Sāhasrī*, dated 1636 AD.

being chased by a man-eating tiger and are extremely afraid and run for your life. As well as experiencing what seems like very real fear, your body will undergo all manner of physiological changes, including increased heart-rate and sweating. Then in your dream one of your fellows who is not being chased shoots and kills the tiger. The sound of

Māyā – 'illusion' – and Śaṅkara's 'two levels of reality'

The term *māyā* is sometimes used in the context of Advaita Vedānta in the sense that conventional reality is 'unreal' or 'illusory'. While some other Advaita Vedāntins did use this term, Śaṅkara did not. Rather, he postulated two 'levels of reality', one absolute and one conventional. Conventional reality is the product of ignorance, *avidyā*. This means that the world we inhabit while ignorant is 'real' at that level; but when ignorance is replaced by knowledge, reality is seen to be different from the conventional world.

In Upaniṣadic terms – for it should be remembered that Śaṅkara was primarily an exegete – conventional reality is 'Brahman with qualities' (*saguṇa Brahman*) and absolute reality is 'qualityless Brahman' (*nirguṇa Brahman*). These expressions are to be found in the *Śvetāśvatara Upaniṣad*. According to this Upaniṣad, among the aspects of 'Brahman with qualities', as well as the conventional world, is a personal Lord. It is often overlooked that Śaṅkara was a theistic monist. He was a devotee of a personal Lord while also holding that ultimately all was one. The positing of the existence of a personal Lord is no more problematic for a monist than are the pluralities around us: ultimately it is all Brahman, personal Lord no less than people and objects.

the dreamed gunshot wakes you up, and at that point you realize that the level of reality of the dream is not the same as the level of reality of your waking state. But your experience both of the chase and of liberation from it derive from the 'less real' level.

Śaṅkara's Advaita Vedānta is perhaps the best known of Indian 'philosophies'. It was the first to be exported to and propounded in the West, being presented by the Vedāntin practitioner Vivekānanda at the World Council of Religions in Chicago in 1893 as 'Hinduism', and subsequently established in various centres, such as 'Rāmakrishna Missions', in many Western countries. It has since enjoyed such a high profile worldwide that not only do outsiders often not realize it is only one among many of India's schools of thought but it is also sometimes promoted as 'the orthodox religio-philosophical tradition of India' within the subcontinent itself.

Rāmānuja: Theist and Philosopher

In fact, more representative of the daily beliefs of many 'Hindus' is the thought of the 11th-century CE Vedāntin, Rāmānuja. Rāmānuja was a fervent member of a highly devotional sect known as the Śrī Vaiṣṇavas, whose object of devotion was the personal Lord as represented in a sectarian text called the *Bhāgavata Purāṇa*. But Rāmānuja also wanted to establish orthodox status for his sect, thereby giving it a superiority over other sects and 'authenticating' his own religious beliefs and practices, and he sought to do this by identifying the theology of the *Bhāgavata Purāṇa* with the ontology and philosophical teachings of the 'triple foundation' of orthodox texts used by Śaṅkara: the *Brahma Sūtra* of Bādarāyaṇa, the Upaniṣads, and the *Bhagavad Gītā*.

Rāmānuja was thus in a position not just of an exegete but also of defender of a specific religious stance. His teachings therefore needed to reconcile these two aspects of his approach. His system of thought, accepted as a branch of the Vedānta darśana as a whole because of the central position it accorded to the Upaniṣads, is known as Viśiṣṭādvaita Vedānta - Vedānta that is non-dual (advaita) but also qualified (*viśiṣṭa*). Unlike Śaṅkara's absolute monism, for Rāmānuja Brahman's oneness is qualified in that there exists within the oneness a relationship between Brahman as Lord (the monism is strongly theistic in Viśiṣṭādvaita Vedānta literature) and the individual self as devotee. Drawing on the rose and redness example used by predecessors, Rāmānuja states that it is the nature of Brahman to exist 'qualified' in this way: as a rose is to its redness, so Brahman is to individual selves. And just as a rose cannot exist without redness (or some other colour), so Brahman cannot exist without selves. These are intrinsic to one another as aspects of

Satkāryavāda – the 'effect pre-exists in the cause'

Satkāryavāda is the theory that nothing can come from nothing – 'creation *ex nihilo*' is impossible. Furthermore, whatever there is must have pre-existed in its material cause, as material causes cannot create something other than what is there in the first place. This theory can be interpreted in different ways. Sāṃkhya, for example, stated that manifest prakṛti pre-existed in unmanifest prakṛti, but that a plurality of puruṣas also existed separate from this. This is satkāryavāda in association with ontological dualism. For Śaṅkara, however, who is an absolute monist, there is nothing that is not unchanging Brahman, and all manifestation and plurality is but an appearance rather than a change in substance. This is known as *vivarta-vāda* – a theory of manifestation by way of 'appearance'. By contrast to these two, Rāmānuja's theory of satkāryavāda, while also monistic like Śaṅkara's, states that Brahman actually transforms itself into the world of plurality. This is known as *pariṇāma-vāda* – a theory of manifestation by way of 'transformation'.

Brahman's nature. Furthermore, these aspects, while not strictly speaking the same thing, are not different from one another either: Rāmānuja does not categorially separate them as the Vaiśeṣikas and Mīmāṃsakas did. Rather, he states that they are intrinsically and eternally inseparable, while also being distinct. This is the meaning of Viśiṣṭādvaita: 'qualified non-dualism'.

Again unlike Śaṅkara, according to Rāmānuja Brahman does not have a qualityless aspect, but is wholly with qualities. This stance is no doubt

According to Rāmānuja, Brahman has qualities:

> Those who maintain [Rāmānuja is here alluding to Śaṅkara] a doctrine of a substratum without any differentiation can offer no valid proof of this, because the objects of all valid means of knowledge are differentiated . . . therefore reality is differentiated and has qualities. . . . [Likewise] the view that all difference is unreal is completely erroneous. . . . Expressions such as *tat tvam asi* [you are all that] in the texts are not meant to convey the unity of undifferentiated substance; on the contrary, the words 'you' and 'that' indicate Brahman characterised by difference.
>
> (Rāmānuja's *Brahma-Sūtra Bhāṣya* 1.1.1)

> The Supreme Brahman – who is a treasure store of countless superlatively auspicious qualities, is flawless, possesses the infinitely great realm manifesting his glory, and is an ocean of superlatively gracious condescension, beauty, and forgiving love – is the principal entity, and the self is the subordinate entity.
>
> (Rāmānuja's *Vedārthasaṃgraha*, quoted in John Carman *Theology of Rāmānuja* p. 152)

partly because sectarian imperatives demand the emphasizing of qualities such as compassion, grace, and so on, as aspects of Brahman. Mention is made of such qualities in some of the Upaniṣads, and Śaṅkara incorporated them into his 'conventional' level theism within an ultimate absolute monism. But Rāmānuja saw these as real and active qualities of the stuff of which the universe is made: the empirical world is a real transformation of Brahman, manifesting qualities, pluralities, and so on that are all ontologically of the same substance. Rāmānuja strongly criticizes Śaṅkara's vivarta-vāda (manifestation by means of appearance) and states that as Brahman is actually the material cause of the empirical world, what is described in the *Chāndoga Upaniṣad* passage 'Being thought to itself, let me become many', is manifestation by means of transformation, *pariṇāma-vāda*. Brahman actually changes, is active, and has a relationship with individuals.

The Logic of the Exegetes

All the Vedic exegetes, whether concerned primarily with the nature and supremacy of the ritual or with the teachings of the Upaniṣads, were faced with the problem of inconsistencies throughout the large corpus of material with which they were working. Though the exegetes believed the texts were records of eternal truth, the ritual manuals and Upaniṣadic treatises were compiled over a vast period of time – possibly more than a millennium. It would thus be extraordinary if they did not contain considerable variations, and even a cursory study of them confirms that this certainly appears to be the case. This allowed different exegetical approaches to be accommodated, and quite different interpretations to have the power to convince in different areas. The attribution to the material, by all of such exegetes, of a status of epistemological certainty (by means of testimony) serves to illustrate an important aspect of the way in which much Indian philosophical thought is inseparable from what in the West would be called a religious worldview. The criticisms of others were frequently presented in logical terms; but they were also frequently founded on a logic internal to a particular system of thought, with arguments directed towards defending a worldview (darśana) which ultimately had soteriological aims. While the different logical arguments can be extrapolated and removed from the context of the tradition as a whole for intellectual interest and for the purposes of comparison with Western forms of logic, the classical Indian context was one in which there was no such formal separation.

Postscript
From Classical Thought to the Modern Day

Just as the high days of pre-Christian Greek philosophy, with its rich tradition of debate, waned over subsequent centuries, so too did the 'classical' period of Indian thought come to a gradual end. If one includes the earliest stages of the tradition, as I have done in this book, it flourished for an astonishing 1500 years – with the first five centuries of the Common Era seeing the greatest activity and variety. The texts and records that have survived to this day attest to very many others that have been lost, or are as yet undiscovered or unexamined, indicating an extraordinarily rich and diverse heritage of original thought and argument. The loss of much of the material is undoubtedly in part due to the fact that there is little or no tradition in India of recording details of historical figures, facts, or events, or of preserving information for a historical record as such. And a great deal of what we do have has survived with almost no information as to its author or origin save for a name, presenting scholars with the huge task, over and above those of editing and translating, of attempting to contextualize it accurately in its tradition. Although much scholarly work has been done to try to piece together biographical facts and chronologies, it is still extremely difficult to be certain about the geographical location in which schools of thought were established, preserved, and taught, to work out how and where it spread, to have anything other than a rough guide as to dates, or to know exactly who wrote which works. Sometimes a name on a text is no more than that – a name. So there is much that we simply do not know about questions of continuity in the Indian tradition, about what happened 'between' parts that we do know, or 'before' or 'after' certain key phases or events about which there is more certainty.

Much of the piecing together of the outline chronology that I have followed in this book was undertaken by pioneer scholars in the field of Indology. As a discipline, this began in the 19th century when a few Western missionaries and travelling academics learned Sanskrit and began editing and translating Indian texts. Many mistakes were made – in particular of the 'looking at Indian material through Western/ Christian eyes' kind – but the early work nevertheless made an enormous contribution to making Indian thought accessible to the West. Work continues around the world, but it remains a comparatively small discipline, and there is still a vast amount of material to be studied properly.

In India itself, until outsiders learned Sanskrit, only a tiny elite were familiar with religio-philosophical material: Sanskrit was the language first of the brahmins, and then of educated 'thinkers', comparable with Latin in medieval Europe. After the classical period waned, there were some areas in which specific philosophical traditions were maintained, if on a less broadly interactive basis. One such that we know about was a 'new' school of Nyāya thought, where classical Nyāya was developed, criticized, and reinterpreted, and on which many further texts were written. Brahmin traditionalists also continued to study and preserve Pāṇini's grammar. What flourished more and were of more influence, however, were strongholds of devotional traditions such as the one Rāmānuja was a member of. Some of these (notably among the Śaiva groups) presented their theistic beliefs as highly sophisticated metaphysical systems, but it was nonetheless the case that cerebral concerns were of interest only to a very small minority. And while Śaṅkara left a legacy of centres where people could put his philosophy into practice, this was for religious exercise rather than as a debating or exegetical forum. Buddhism survived only outside India, in countries such as China, Tibet, Japan, Sri Lanka, Myanmar (Burma), and Thailand. Scholarly Buddhists, particularly in Tibet, continued to engage in the more philosophical issues within their own schools of Buddhism, but the tradition endured largely as a religion.

In many respects, it was the interest of outsiders that triggered a self-conscious revival among many less 'popular' Indian traditions. Seeing that others were learning Sanskrit, seeking out and editing texts, and wanting to know about the history of the ideas of India, prompted Indians to resume a more active interest in their own classical traditions. Some did this with the aim of promoting their own particular tradition much as had been done in the past. This was the case particularly with Śaṅkara's Advaita Vedānta, which very successfully presented itself in a simplified form for Western consumption. This form is mainly of interest to Westerners whose concern is its soteriology. In India too, the focus of the Śaṅkara centres remains largely practical.

It has been educational establishments in India (many of which were established by the British in the 19th century) that have provided the milieu in which Indian philosophy flourished again during the 20th century. Professional Indian scholars joined Western scholars in studying the classical texts and, in university departments in India and the West alike, debate has resumed on the relative merits of different systems of thought, their internal coherence, the validity of their arguments, the strengths or weaknesses of their methodologies. In broad terms, this has been undertaken in a variety of disciplines, as scholars approach the material from different angles. Philologists, historians, students of religion, and philosophers have each raised different kinds of questions and contributed to modern debate in different ways.

Because of the influence of Western ways of doing things, however, there has also been a tendency to separate philosophy in the sense of rational argument from any context that incorporated more religious issues. So in India as in the West, Indian philosophy in a more specific sense has become an academic discipline concerned primarily with logic and linguistic analysis. In order to be taken seriously on the international stage of modern Western philosophy, it has had to compete only on those terms that are of interest to modern Western philosophers. Drawing mainly on the work of Naiyāyikas and Buddhists, some have devoted their professional careers to promoting Indian philosophy strictly in the sense of logical argument – in order to overcome Western preconceptions that Indian thought is 'mystical', 'magical', and anything but rational. Rationality, many thought (and many still think), was the province only of the West. While one must applaud any successful overcoming of such misconceptions, it is also to be hoped that before too long professional philosophers will be less reluctant to pay due attention to the wider context in which Indian logic was developed, and the reasons why it was developed: its total abstraction from context is a wholly Western cultural phenomenon. With its fundamental focus on the nature of reality itself, much more profound than this was the worldview of classical India.

Recommended further reading

Chapter 1

Simon Blackburn, *Think*, Oxford: OUP, 1999.

Sarandranath Dasgupta, *A History of Indian Philosophy*, Delhi: Motilal Banarsidass, 1975.

Paul Dundas, *The Jains*, London: Routledge, 1992.

Eric Frauwallner, *History of Indian Philosophy*, Delhi: Motilal Banarsidass, 1993.

John Hospers, *Introduction to Philosophical Analysis* (3rd edn), London: Routledge, 1990.

The chapter on Śaivism in S. Sutherland et al. (eds) *The World's Religions*, London: Routledge, 1988.

Chapter 2

J. L. Brockington, *The Sacred Thread*, Edinburgh: Edinburgh University Press, 1981.

Thomas J. Hopkins, *The Hindu Religious Tradition*, Belmont, CA: Wadsworth Publishing Company, 1971.

R. E. Hume, Introductory essay in *The Thirteen Principal Upanishads* (2nd edn), Delhi: Oxford University Press, 1931.

Wendy Doniger O'Flaherty, (ed. and trans.) *The Rig Veda: An Anthology*, Harmondsworth: Penguin, 1981.

Patrick Olivelle, (trans.) *Upaniṣads*, Oxford: Oxford University Press, 1996.

B. K. Smith, *Classifying the Universe: The Ancient Indian Varṇa System and the Origins of Caste*, Oxford: Oxford University Press, 1994.

Chapter 3

Rupert Gethin, *The Foundations of Buddhism*, Oxford: Oxford University Press, 1998.

Richard Gombrich, *Theravāda Buddhism: A Social History from Benares to Colombo*, London: Routledge and Kegan Paul, 1988.

Sue Hamilton, *Early Buddhism – A New Approach: The I of the Beholder*, Richmond: Curzon Press, 2000.

Damien Keown, *Buddhism: A Very Short Introduction*, Oxford: Oxford University Press, 1996.

Walpola Rahula, *What the Buddha Taught* (2nd edn), London: Gordon Fraser, 1967.

Andrew Skilton, *A Concise History of Buddhism*, Birmingham: Windhorse Publications, 1994.

Complete translations of the texts of early Buddhism are published by the Pali Text Society. Alternatives for some sections are:

Bhikkhu Ñāṇamoli and Bhikkhu Bodhi, (translation of the *Majjhima Nikāya*) *The Middle Length Discourses of the Buddha*, Boston: Wisdom Publications in association with the Barre Centre for Buddhist Studies, 1995.

Maurice Walshe, (translation of the *Dīgha Nikāya*) *Thus Have I Heard*, London: Wisdom Publications, 1987.

Chapter 4

There is almost no non-specialist reading material on this period. Some general references are made in:

Harold G. Coward and K. Kunjunni Raja, *Encyclopedia of Indian Philosophies*, Vol. V: *The Philosophy of the Grammarians*, Delhi: Motilal Banarsidass, 1990.

W. Halbfass, *India and Europe: An Essay in Understanding*, Albany, NY: State University of New York Press, 1988.

Richard King, *Indian Philosophy: An Introduction to Hindu and Buddhist Thought*, Edinburgh: Edinburgh University Press, 1999.

J. N. Mohanty, *Classical Indian Philosophy*, New York: Rowman and Littlefield, 2000.

More specialized:

George Cardona, 'Indian Linguistics', in Giulio Lepschy (ed.) *History of Linguistics*, Vol. I: *The Eastern Traditions of Linguistics*, London: Longman, 1994.

B. K. Matilal, *Logic, Language and Reality*, Delhi: Motilal Banarsidass, 1985.

Chapter 5

E. Frauwallner, *History of Indian Philosophy*, Vol. II, Delhi: Motilal Banarsidass, 1973.

M. Hiriyanna, *The Essentials of Indian Philosophy*, London: George Allen & Unwin, 1985.

Richard King, *Indian Philosophy: An Introduction to Hindu and Buddhist Thought*, Edinburgh: Edinburgh University Press, 1999.

J. N. Mohanty, *Classical Indian Philosophy*, New York: Rowman and Littlefield, 2000.

More specialized:

Wilhelm Halbfass, *On Being and What There Is: Classical Vaiśeṣika and the History of Indian Ontology*, Albany, NY: State University of New York Press, 1992.

B. K. Matilal, *Perception: An Essay on Classical Indian Theories of Knowledge*, Oxford: Clarendon Press, 1986.

Chapter 6

Stefan Anacker, *Seven Works of Vasubandhu: The Buddhist Psychological Doctor*, Delhi: Motilal Banarsidass, 1984.

Ian Harris, *The Continuity of Madhyamaka and Yogācāra in Indian Mahāyāna Buddhism*, Leiden: E. J. Brill, 1991.
C. W. Huntingdon, *The Emptiness of Emptiness. An Introduction to Early Indian Mādhyamika*, Honolulu: University of Hawaii Press, 1989.
Richard King, *Indian Philosophy: An Introduction to Hindu and Buddhist Thought*, Edinburgh: Edinburgh University Press, 1999.
Thomas A. Kochumuttom, *A Buddhist Doctrine of Experience*, Delhi: Motilal Banarsidass, 1982.
F. Th. Stcherbatsky, *Buddhist Logic*, New York: Dover Publications, 1962.
Frederick Streng, *Emptiness. A Study in Religious Meaning*, Nashville, TN: Abingdon Press, 1967.
Paul Williams, *Mahāyāna Buddhism: The Doctrinal Foundations*, London: Routledge, 1989.

More specialized:
Shoryu Katsura, (ed.), *Dharmakīrti's Thought and its Impact on Indian and Tibetan Philosophy*. Proceedings of the Third International Dharmakīrti Conference, Hiroshima, November 4–6, 1997. Vienna: Österreichische Akademie der Wissenschaften, 1999.

Chapter 7

Georg Feuerstein, *The Yoga-Sūtra of Patañjali: A New Translation and Commentary*, Folkestone: Dawson, 1979.
Georg Feuerstein, *The Philosophy of Classical Yoga*, Manchester: Manchester University Press, 1980.
Richard King, *Indian Philosophy: An Introduction to Hindu and Buddhist Thought*, Edinburgh: Edinburgh University Press, 1999.
Gerald Larson, *Classical Sāṃkhya* (2nd edn), Delhi: Motilal Banarsidass, 1979.
Ian Whicher, *The Integrity of the Yoga Darśana: A Reconsideration of Classical Yoga*, Albany, NY: State University of New York Press, 1998.
J. H. Woods, *The Yoga System of Patañjali*, Cambridge, MA: Harvard University Press, 1983.

Chapter 8

A. J. Alston, (trans.) *The Thousand Teachings of Śaṅkara*, London: Shanti Sadan, 1990.

Ashok Aklujkar, 'Summary of Bhartṛhari's Vākyapadīya' in Karl H. Potter (ed.) *Encyclopedia of Indian Philosophies*, Delhi: Motilal Banarsidass, 1991.

John Carman, *Theology of Rāmānuja*, New Haven, CT: Yale University Press, 1974.

Eliot Deutsch, *Advaita Vedānta: A Philosophical Reconstruction*, Honolulu: University of Hawaii Press, 1968.

M. Hiriyanna, *Essentials of Indian Philosophy*, London: George, Allen & Unwin, 1985.

Richard King, *Indian Philosophy: An Introduction to Hindu and Buddhist Thought*, Edinburgh: Edinburgh University Press, 1999.

J. N. Mohanty, *Classical Indian Philosophy*, New York: Rowman and Littlefield, 2000.

George Thibaut, (trans.) *The Vedānta-Sūtras with the Commentary of Śaṅkarācārya*, ed. Max Müller, *Sacred Books of the East Series*, Vols. XXXIV and XXXVIII, Oxford: Clarendon Press, 1890 and 1896.

George Thibaut, (trans.) *The Vedānta-Sūtras with the Commentary of Rāmānuja*, ed. Max Müller, Sacred Books of the East Series, Vol. XLVIII, Oxford: Clarendon Press, 1904.

Other recommended books

A. L. Basham, *The Wonder that was India: A Survey of the Indian Subcontinent before the Coming of the Muslims*, London: Sidgwick and Jackson, 1954.

Franklin Edgerton, *The Beginnings of Indian Philosophy: Selections from the Ṛg Veda, Atharva Veda, Upaniṣads, and Mahābhārata*, London: Allen and Unwin, 1965.

Jonardon Ganeri, (ed.) *Indian Logic: A Reader*, Richmond: Curzon Press, 2000

J. N. Mohanty, *Reason and Tradition in Indian Thought*, Oxford: Clarendon Press, 1992.

Wilhelm Halbfass, *Tradition and Reflection: Explorations in Indian Thought*, Albany, NY: SUNY Press, 1991.

Karl Potter, *Presuppositions of India's Philosophies*, Delhi: Motilal Banarsidass, 1991.

Karl Potter, (ed.) *Encyclopedia of Indian Philosophies*, Delhi: Motilal Banarsidass, 1970–93.

S. Radhakrishnan and C. A. Moore, *A Sourcebook in Indian Philosophy*, Princeton, NJ: Princeton University Press, 1957.

Ninian Smart, *Doctrine and Argument in Indian Philosophy*, London: George Allen & Unwin, 1964.

Index

A

B

C

D

E

O

P

Q

R

71. Choice Theory
72. Architecture
73. Poststructuralism
74. Postmodernism
75. Democracy
76. Empire
77. Fascism
78. Terrorism
79. Plato
80. Ethics
81. Emotion
82. Northern Ireland
83. Art Theory
84. Locke
85. Modern Ireland
86. Globalization
87. Cold War
88. The History of Astronomy
89. Schizophrenia
90. The Earth
91. Engels
92. British Politics
93. Linguistics
94. The Celts
95. Ideology
96. Prehistory
97. Political Philosophy
98. Postcolonialism
99. Atheism
100. Evolution
101. Molecules
102. Art History
103. Presocratic Philosophy
104. The Elements
105. Dada and Surrealism
106. Egyptian Myth
107. Christian Art

BUDDHA

A Very Short Introduction

Michael Carrithers

Michael Carrithers guides us through the diverse accounts of the life and teaching of the Buddha. He discusses the social and political background of India in the Buddha's time, and traces the development of his thought. He also assesses the rapid and widespread assimilation of Buddhism and its relevance today.

'admirably well-paced and informative'

Sunday Times

www.oup.co.uk/isbn/0-19-285453-4

ANCIENT PHILOSOPHY

A Very Short Introduction

Julia Annas

The tradition of ancient philosophy is a long, rich and varied one, in which a constant note is that of discussion and argument. This book aims to introduce readers to some ancient debates and to get them to engage with the ancient developments of philosophical themes. Getting away from the presentation of ancient philosophy as a succession of Great Thinkers, the book aims to give readers a sense of the freshness and liveliness of ancient philosophy, and of its wide variety of themes and styles.

> 'Incisive, elegant, and full of the excitement of doing philosophy, Julia Annas's Short Introduction boldly steps outside of conventional chronological ways of organizing material about the Greeks and Romans to get right to the heart of the human problems that exercised them, problems ranging from the relation between reason and emotion to the objectivity of truth. I can't think of a better way to begin.'
>
> **Martha Nussbaum, University of Chicago**

www.oup.co.uk/vsi/ancientphilosophy

CONTINENTAL PHILOSOPHY

A Very Short Introduction

Simon Critchley

Continental philosophy is a contested concept which cuts to the heart of the identity of philosophy and its relevance to matters of public concern and personal life. This book attempts to answer the question 'What is Continental philosophy?' by telling a story that began with Kant 200 years ago and includes discussions of major philosophers like Nietzsche, Husserl and Heidegger. At the core of the book is a plea to place philosophy at the centre of cultural life, and thus reawaken its ancient definition of the love of wisdom that makes life worth living.

> 'Antagonism and mutual misrepresentation between so-called analytical and continental philosophy have helped shape the course of every significant development in Western intellectual life since the 1960s – structuralism, post-structuralism, postmodernism, gender studies, etc. Simon Critchley has skilfully and sympathetically sketched continental lines of thought so that strangers to their detail may enter them systematically enough that their principle texts begin to illuminate one another. It is a remarkable achievement.'

Stanley Cavell, Harvard University

www.oup.co.uk/isbn/0-19-285359-7